Welcome Aboard!

Your Career As A Flight Attendant

BECKY S. BOCK

with
Cheryl A. Cage

Published by Cage Consulting, Inc.
Please come visit our Website!
http://www.cageconsulting.com

Welcome Aboard! Your Career as a Flight Attendant
by Becky S. Bock

with contributions by Cheryl A. Cage which include:
Flight Attendant Self-Evaluation Worksheet
Paperwork Presentation
Conducting a Mock Interview
Types of Interviews

Editing by Cheryl A. Cage, Pam Ryan, Marcia Konegni.
Cover Design and Book Layout by Bobbi Benson, Benson Communications.
Author Photo by Pat Harrison, Keane and Harrison.
Cover picture by Real Life Photo/Stock Imagery.

Printed in the United States of America.
Published by Cage Consulting, Inc.

Library of Congress Catalog Card Number 97-078405
ISBN 0-9642839-3-X

To Terry.

*Without your constant encouragement, confidence, and
incredible computer skills this book could never be.*

Acknowledgements

Many thanks to the airline personnel of American Airlines,
American Eagle, United Airlines, USAirways, and TWA for being
accessible with their time and information.

Also my thanks go to Kevin Horan, American Eagle, for his
information and input with the Brief History chapter.

To Cheryl Cage for consistently helpful comments and
encouragement as well as her professionalism.

Table Of Contents

Definitions And Considerations

Aviation Terms

There are many words unique to a flight attendant position and the airline industry. It is awkward to explain the definition of each word when it is used in the text of this book. For this reason we have included an extensive glossary of terms at the back of this book. If you come upon a term that is unfamiliar to you please refer to the Glossary for a definition.

Considerations

For reasons of clarity and because this book is written for both male and female flight attendant hopefuls, we have alternated the use of masculine and feminine pronouns throughout the book.

Foreword

Who hasn't sat in an airport terminal people watching? Among the people you notice most often are flight attendants. Whether it is an impressive sight, or an embarrassing one, depends on the degree of professionalism with which those flight attendants conduct themselves. A flight attendant's job is not conducted solely on an airplane. Walking through an airport, eating in an airport restaurant, or simply waiting in the boarding area a flight attendant is often the traveling public's first impression of the airline. Was it a good impression or an unpleasant one?

As you will see, on and off the aircraft, a flight attendant is the example to the public of an image the airline wishes to impart. You can be certain the image desired is one of a professional.

This book will help to prepare you for your Flight Attendant interviews and, ultimately, your Flight Attendant career. Understanding the job and its responsibilities will better enable you to achieve this career. Yes, career, because that is exactly what you can expect when you are hired as today's Flight Attendant.

Notes

Chapter 1
A Brief History

Many important and impressive inventions can be associated with the turn of the century, but few can compare to the success, popularity and impact on future generations as the airplane.

As ordinary as mail service seems today, utilizing the airplane to fly the U.S. mail caused tremendous advances in aviation. (At that time flights were conducted only during daylight as it was considered unsafe to fly in darkness.)

The gradual addition of paying passengers happened shortly thereafter. Often the only seat available was on top of the mail bags. Passengers boarded with the excitement of entering a new frontier. The issuance of helmets, goggles, and parachutes added to the thrill.

The 1920s and 1930s are credited with another notable beginning — that of the founding of the "Big Four" airlines: Eastern Air Lines, United Air Lines, American Airlines, and Transcontinental/Western Airlines.

The inflight service was meager if at all. It could consist of the copilot serving apples, coffee from a thermos and possibly a sandwich. Assistance was non-existent if a passenger needed first aid, an airsick bag, or a restroom!

Western Air Express hired male couriers in 1929 to calm passengers and see to their comfort. Pan American hired male stewards. Their duties were to serve refreshments and to look after the well-being of their passengers. To the airlines, steward was an acronym for "Service, Tact, Efficiency, Wisdom, Ability, Responsibility, Dependability." Additional requirements included that he be an American citizen, speak three languages fluently (including English and French), be a high school graduate, have experience in both preparing and serving food in a first class hotel, restaurant, or steamship, and that he have a good aptitude and personality for handling people.

Training back then was completed in two months: five weeks of basic first aid training followed by a course in advanced first aid; two to three weeks of assisting in the equipping of aircraft for passenger service as well as apprenticing with a senior steward to learn galley procedures, how to make up berths, and emergency skills. Included in their duties were: checking in luggage and mail, making up the passenger lists, completing weight reports and, of course, greeting and making the passengers comfortable. After a 60-day probation, he was then allowed to go to Bermuda as a working crew member. After his proficiency was attained, he proceeded on the transatlantic routes as a fully "trained and graduated" steward.

1930s

A young, outgoing, female aviation enthusiast entered the all male dominated airline world. Ellen Church made an appointment with Mr. Steve Stimpson, the district manager of Boeing Air Transport, inquiring about a possible job. Initially, her heart was set on being a copilot, but through her discussions with Mr. Stimpson and the fact that there was a growing need for passenger care, they decided a woman's touch might be an added boost for the flying public. Ellen suggested that nurses fill these positions. Having women on board would add the psychological bonus of demonstrating that flying was indeed a safe and reliable form of transportation. The response from the top was a definitive "No." Mr. Stimpson persevered and in time received the go-ahead to hire eight "Stewardesses" on a 3-month trial basis.

Like the stewards who flew before them, stewardesses had job requirements as well. They were hired on the basis of personality, intelligence, and marital status. Because of the small aircraft, narrow aisles, and low ceiling, height and weight restrictions were established: 115 pounds and 5'4" were the absolute maximums! At age 25 they were required to retire. The salary was $125.00 a month for 100 hours of flight time; an extra $5.00 if delayed or stuck because of weather.

The image of the nurse was carried out visually as well as theoretically. While serving meals, stewardesses were required to wear white nurses' uniforms and caps. One of the original group, Inez Fieler Fuite, said "passengers couldn't wait to meet her, touch her, and touch the aircraft." They were called "The White Angels from the Sky."

With the obvious success of the first stewardesses, other airlines soon followed suit, and hired female inflight help.

1940s

With the 1940s came World War II and its war effort and demands. Nurses were greatly needed outside of aviation. The requirement of nurse was dropped and other requirements took its place: single women, certain age, dimensions of height and weight, 20/20 vision and college graduate or public service experience. The glamorous image of the stewardess emerged in spite of low salaries and absolutely no job security. The desire to become a "stew" was high and only a very select few filled the positions. On the average, a stewardess stayed on the job for two years or until she married.

By the late 1940s each stewardess was required by her employer to sign a contract agreeing to quit by the age of 32. Around this same time, a United Airlines stewardess, D.A. Brown, began organizing stewardesses into their first bargaining unit with the assistance of the Air Line Pilots Association (ALPA - which is still in force today). Within the first two months of organizing, almost all United Airlines stewardesses were registered members of the first Airline Stewardess Association. The unionization of stewardesses was just the beginning of many successful, powerful, and necessary unions to come. Without unions the flight attendants of today would not, in all probability, be able to fly to a normal retirement age of 65 and, in some cases, even longer.

1950s

A sample of an American Airlines' recruiting brochure: "You're in for the thrill of your life when you finally get your assignment. The cabin is your castle. You'll be working aboard great DC-7's, DC-6's or Convairs — the most modern fleet in the world."

During this era the first official stewardess college was dedicated with the emphasis in training being in airplane safety, food service, and medical emergencies.

1960s

This period is notable for its changes of uniforms. However, unnoticeable to the public eye were the separate seniority lists that were in effect for men and women. Men could marry and have children while the women had to remain single and childless.

With the victorious Civil Rights Act of 1964 prohibiting discrimination on the basis of race, sex, age, or marital status came the revision of job requirements and training. The term "flight attendant" was adopted to replace steward and stewardess. Both sexes would now fall under one title as well as one set of rules and regulations.

1970s-1980s

Along with deregulation came a huge demand for flight attendants. The airlines couldn't seem to train and equip the new hires fast enough. The male flight attendant population during these years was growing quickly. It was becoming commonplace to see not just one man, but often an entire male crew on board. It seems things had come full circle: Whereas in years before it was felt a woman's presence created a trusting and secure environment in the cabin, men were now playing that same role. The training programs continued to emphasize customer service and welfare, but passenger security was given as much attention and priority in training as it was in the media. Flight attendants began performing the complex job of coupling "service with a smile" and safety with trained confidence. During these years crews now had to be prepared for the possibilities of bomb threats, hijackings, and even physical attacks from the traveling public.

1990s and Beyond

As more airlines merge and vie for passengers' loyalties, these same companies are rethinking the standards previously set. Gone is the "must retire by age 32", as more and more flight attendants continue to work into their 30s, 40s, 50s, and, yes, even 60s and 70s.

Flight attendants continue to make history with the assistance of federal regulations and union negotiations. Dedicated men and women are making this a career from which to retire, and the flying public continues to benefit from their professionalism.

So, whether you are married, have a family, are single, or just desire a career change the future for the flight attendant career field looks brighter than ever before!

Notes

Chapter 2
A Reserve Story

Receiving "the call" from scheduling with a trip assignment is my first step to getting on board an aircraft as a working flight attendant. I had my bags packed and uniforms ready the evening before, so it would be a smooth transition from home to airport. I've been assigned a three-day trip with an early return to my home domicile on the last day.

At my airline check-in is one hour prior to our scheduled departure time. Flight attendants are given up to a 10-minute grace period after the scheduled check-in. If I am later than this, I will be replaced with someone else and my airline has possible grounds for termination. Being on time and dependable is vital for a flight attendant.

My check-in is accomplished in the crew room via the computer. It has taken time to learn the system my airline uses. I print out the entire crew list as well as the trip pairing. I also check my mail file for manual updates, bulletins, and company correspondence. It's important to keep my eye on my watch and my crew; I would hate for everyone else to leave for the aircraft without me. I find my crew gathering and preparing for our briefing which is led by the captain. This briefing covers crew coordination expectations during normal operations as well as in the event of an emergency. The captain also briefs us on any pertinent information she may have concerning inflight weather and flight times. This briefing has provided me the opportunity to meet the people I will be working with for the next three days. The flight attendant crew is very senior to me and I feel a bit intimidated.

After the briefing is complete, we gather our crew luggage and head for the gate where our aircraft awaits. Walking through the airport as an entire crew feels really good. I remember watching crews before I was hired and imagining all sorts of exciting lifestyles. I can hardly believe I am now a part of this group of professionals.

Once we're all on board the aircraft we stow our luggage and the lead flight attendant establishes our duty positions and we go into action. Being on reserve often means getting the least desirable position to work. However, on this trip, like many others, two of the flight attendants (Cheryl and Donna) are friends and want to work together, thus leaving a more desirable position open to me. This trip I am assigned to the aft area of the aircraft. My responsibilities will be: keeping the inventory of the catering, liquor and liquor money, and working the beverage cart. Carol, my aft co-worker, will ensure the video system (used for the safety video and inflight movie) is set up and operating. While she checks the video equipment I check all the emergency equipment in my designated area. We also check the aft lavatories to ensure the smoke detectors are working.

I then focus on the catering. Working the aft portion of the airplane means I am responsible for receiving the coach class and special request meals and making sure all appropriate beverages are loaded on board. Carol checks over the order form as I visually check that the list and the meals agree. Often, problems may arise inflight concerning a special request meal that was signed for by the flight attendant but failed to make its way to the airplane. Mid-flight is not a good time to catch a mistake! It can make a difference in a passenger's overall enjoyment of a flight and his impression of the airline and its crew. I try hard to make sure before takeoff that the meals and the passenger head count are in synch.

Because my flight attendant position is in the rear of the airplane, during boarding I can observe the passengers as they arrive. I need to keep an eye on luggage storage and people having difficulty finding their assigned seats. In the case of a double seat assignment, I inform the lead flight attendant of the problem. If I can't physically make my way up front, I call her on the interphone to give the information needed to correct the problem. It's very important to correct the situation. It can and does happen that someone is on the wrong flight! Good communication between the front and the back of the airplane is vital.

I happen to notice a man hauling an oversized musical case down the aisle. My first thought is "No way! How on earth did it get past the gate agent and the flight attendant at the entry door?" I assist the passenger the best I can. The case clearly will not fit in the overhead bin or under the seat in front of him. I tell him it must be checked and placed in the baggage compartment under the aircraft. The passenger is completely against this idea, so I mention he would be welcome to pay a 1/2 fare ticket and, room permitting, we could strap it into a window seat next to him. Problem solved!

Now that the boarding process is complete, we must have a correct head count of the passengers. I find myself counting three times just to ensure it is correct. Carol has followed behind me closing overhead bins and also taking a count. Since this flight is almost full, I have learned a little trick from Carol: Count the empty seats. I'll remember this and use it in the future — anything to make this job easier.

We agree on the final count and pass the number on to the boarding agent and the cockpit crew. We cannot close the entry or cockpit doors until this is done. The number of passengers and the number of tickets must match as security is a very big concern. The lead flight attendant makes the "Flight Attendants Prepare for Departure" announcement. We arm our doors and the aircraft is pushed back from the gate area by the ground crew. As we taxi toward the takeoff runway the lead flight attendant also gives the "Welcome Aboard" PA. The airplane we are on has overhead television monitors so the lead flight attendant begins the passenger pre-flight and emergency procedures video. These demonstrations are not to meet just the airline's standards but the FAA's as well. With the final seat belt, luggage, and cabin readiness for takeoff checks complete, the flight attendants prepare for departure by strapping themselves into the jumpseats.

As soon as possible after takeoff, and by that I mean when it's safe to do so, we are all out of our seats and on to the next phase of our jobs. Often we are up before the "Fasten Seat Belt" sign has been turned off. I've had to become accustomed to standing and working at all angles of climb and descent. It's often referred to as "getting your sea legs." The sea legs." The beverage cart is now the focus of Carol's and my attention and, with that, the preparation for the beverage and meal service. Cheryl (the lead flight attendant who is working in the forward, normally first-class, cabin) begins selling headsets to those passengers who wish to watch the movie. Donna begins serving the first-class passengers beverages and snacks.

As Carol and I begin the service, I feel as though I'm in everybody's way. The galley area is a very small area to work in. Add to this small space a 200+ pound beverage cart, two and sometimes three flight attendants, and the probability that a passenger will want to come aft and either use the restroom or stand and talk, you can imagine how crowded it can become. We work hard at maintaining a pleasant demeanor while dodging and squeezing around each other. I find it amusing that as soon as the "Fasten Seat Belt" sign is turned off, so many people want to stand up or use the lavatories. We excuse ourselves as we make our way with the beverage cart up and down the aisle. Carol checks for feet sticking out, I look for arms in the aisle. To have the beverage cart run over your foot or hit your arm can be painful! We must time our beverage service so when we are halfway through the cabin, the meal service can begin. The meal cart from the forward galley is used first and by the time that meal cart is empty, our initial beverage service is complete and we can bring out the aft galley meal cart to complete the meal distribution.

Before the meal service is initiated, Cheryl has checked my manifest for special meal requests. There are always a few "specials" (as they are referred to by the crew). Whether they are "kids' meals," low fat, vegetarian, kosher, or any other special request, matching the passenger with the meal must be done ahead of the regular meals. Often a passenger forgets he ordered a special meal at the time of making a reservation for the flight and will accept a regular meal, thus shorting our supply to the remaining passengers. Then we may end up with a vegetarian meal that may not satisfy the child sitting in the last row. We try very hard to see that everyone is happy with their inflight meal selection. This, in itself, is a big accomplishment!

Once the video headsets are distributed, the first beverage service is completed, and the meals are all passed out, we must re-stock the cart for the second beverage service. Carol and I begin the service while

Cheryl begins trash pickup prior to collecting the meal trays. (Picking up loose trash such as cups, cans, etc. makes it easier to stack the trays back in the meal cart.) As we offer seconds of the beverages, invariably many of the passengers try to hand me their meal tray. Carol asks Cheryl to please make a PA informing everyone that the trays will be collected shortly and to please hold on to them until we can come through after the beverages are offered. By this time, everyone wants to get out of their seats, stretch in the aisle, or line up for the restroom again. I notice the last row aisle-seated passengers have it worse than us — the people are almost standing in their faces! I offer these people a free cocktail for the inconvenience. We try to have the movie going by now. That usually helps cut down on a lot of congestion for as long as it's playing.

Speaking of inconvenience, Cheryl has just informed us (via the interphone) that we are probably going to have a delay due to weather at our destination. The captain will speak to everyone and keep us informed as she receives updates from Air Traffic Control. Sure enough, the Captain's voice comes over the PA (interrupting the movie) and she explains that, due to bad weather in the area, we will have to enter a holding pattern until conditions improve or a diversion to an alternate airport is required.

We hold, and hold, and hold. The weather is not improving and there are many airplanes ahead of us waiting to land. Because of these facts, the captain decides to land at an alternate airport where the weather is better and we can land right away.

In the cabin, we've been fielding questions such as: "Will I make my connection?", "What happens if we divert?", "My boyfriend's waiting for me at LaGuardia (NY). What's going to happen?" We have unaccompanied minors traveling alone, many passengers trying to connect with other flights, and no word yet from the company on the plans to handle the passengers problems once we land. We continue to hand out pillows, blankets, coffee, water, and as much empathy as humanly possible! I, too, want to be in problems—I've never been to New York!

The decision to land in Newark, New Jersey, and bus the passengers to LaGuardia has been announced to everyone. Audible moans and groans are heard throughout the cabin. This diversion in itself can add anywhere from three to four hours to an already trying day.

The approach into Newark is turbulent and I hear a few nervous exclamations. The passengers are keeping a watchful eye to see my reactions to each and every bump. I keep my expressions even and unconcerned and make sure I smile at every passenger that looks to me for reassurance. It is easy to smile because I am confident in the skills of our pilots.

After landing, sighs of relief are heard throughout the cabin. In fact, some even applaud! As we taxi up to the jetway area, the flight attendant call lights begin to illuminate — questions and concerns must be dealt with. Cheryl makes a PA telling everyone that as soon as the passenger service agent arrives on board, more information will be provided. "Please remain seated."

With the arrival of the agent and the buses, an orderly deplaning is accomplished. The final good-byes and assistance with luggage and personal belongings are completed. It is now the flight crew's turn to see what scheduling wants to do with us. We don't ride on the bus with the passengers; we are instructed to take a taxi to our overnight hotel. We need to be "in position" for the following day's series of flights, so we, too, endure the freeways and infamous New York traffic.

By the time we arrive at our hotel we are all visibly tired and ready for a decent night's sleep — so much for my exciting first night in glamorous New York! I'm tired and hungry and without an ounce of energy for anything more than taking a shower.

The captain completes the crew check-in to the hotel, hands each of us our respective room key, and confirms our hotel departure time. We all agree as to the time to meet in the lobby, enter the elevator together and ascend to our floors. After our goodnights are said, I enter my room. The silence of my room is so comforting. I feel as though I've been talking for days instead of only 13 hours. I can't wait to get out of my uniform and into a shower. As I prepare for bed, I turn on the TV to check tomorrow's forecast — more of the same weather problems for New York. I'm just relieved we will be heading south tomorrow. Miami appears to be clear and sunny and that's our next city. However, I'm already learning to stay flexible. We still have two more days and five more flights scheduled. Anything can happen in that amount of time!

A CONVERSATION WITH A NEW-HIRE (2 Months!)
RESERVE FLIGHT ATTENDANT

I recently had a conversation with a new-hire reserve flight attendant. She shared some of her fears and excitement about her new career.

She is terrified of the "quick call." She lives 47 miles from the airport and is afraid she will not make it to work in the allotted time. Moving closer to her domicile seems inevitable.

She finds it uncomfortable not knowing what her status for the following morning will be. Will she be called for a trip or just sit around waiting for the phone to ring? Because of this she wakes up at 2:00am to shower and wash her hair, and then goes back to bed! She has been told by seasoned flight crew members that she will develop a "feel" for the reserve information (how many trips are open for the next day, how many reserves are available, etc.) so she will have a better idea when she might get called out for a trip.

She LOVES her work. The company has her on a very short leash but she doesn't mind at all. She is in her mid-40s and is willing to do everything to make this her career. She has found her co-workers very kind, helpful, and friendly. She feels fortunate that she is finally able to fulfill a lifelong dream.

Notes

Chapter 3
Job Description

I magine having the ability to convey an image of professionalism to hundreds of men, women, and children in a single day. You command the attention and respect of people who, without knowing you personally, trust you.

As a flight attendant, the impression you make will be a lasting one. That impression could be the reason for a customer who returns rather than one who flies off with the competition.

BEING PHYSICALLY PREPARED

How do your prepare yourself for the inevitable 14-hour days and short overnights? You can't possibly go into training as you would if running a marathon was your goal. However, being a flight attendant does require a higher degree of health and stamina than most other careers. Being on your feet for hours, to return the following day to begin again is not something that can be taught in textbooks. Like anything else that is physically challenging, endurance must be built up over time.

Each major airline, as well as the small airlines, will test your medical condition before you are offered employment. Your application will also require a truthful disclosure of any existing medical problems. The airline may want to review your medical records. A follow-up exam could be ordered depending upon any medical questions that arise.

However, something that cannot be inspected is your future health once on the line. You will be in direct and indirect contact with hundreds of people from all over the world on each flight. Direct, by picking up used cups and service items; indirect, by breathing the recirculated air of each and every person on board. I was amazed at how many colds I caught my first year as a flight attendant. I soon realized how important my health was to my career.

I found taking care of myself a priority more than ever before. Vitamins became a part of my daily routine. Sleep was and still is of vital importance to one's well-being and disposition. The passengers have paid the price of a ticket and deserve a flight crew well rested, healthy, and in a good mood. They should not have to pay the added high price of a flight attendant's poor judgment from the night before. Government and airline companies have passed regulations regarding alcohol and drug consumption. Required rest times between duty periods have also been addressed. However, common sense cannot be regulated. It is entirely up to the flight attendant to know his or her own personal health requirements, and make sure they are followed.

Exercise is a powerful plus when applied to this career. You don't get energy just from proper nutrition. If I could run, walk, or swim during a layover, instead of being exhausted the next day, I found the exercise gave me the extra energy I needed as well as a boost in emotional well-being. The passengers and your crewmembers are on the receiving end of your improved demeanor. The union's Hotel Committee assessment of a hotel's desirability often includes the availability of a workout room as well as the accessibility of restaurants.

Some people love airplane food. For a new-hire on a tight budget, having meals on the airplane may appear to be a desirable alternative to having to purchase food. I started with an airline that did not provide meals. Peanuts got old very quickly. Packing my own food and water became second nature. I knew how easy it could become to give in to the temptation of airport fast food and vending machines. I decided early in my career that eating properly was a responsibility to myself, my crew, and the passengers. I refused to allow snacks, cookies, and candy bars to become a diet staple. I knew it was just a matter of time before I would succumb to the headaches and energy decline that are inevitable with that type of diet. I can remember the remarks from some fellow flight attendants concerning how "good" I was to resist. I knew the importance of feeling my best and the relation of good health to my job performance. I wasn't being "good," I was being a conscientious employee.

Being prepared physically and emotionally will always benefit you, your company, your co-workers, and, especially, the passengers!

LONG HOURS, SHORT NOTICES

The long "on duty" hours that a flight attendant works need to be explained and emphasized. Airlines run 24 hours a day, 365 days a year. This includes holidays. If having Thanksgiving and Christmas with your family and friends is of great importance to you, you might want to rethink your priorities before you submit an application for a flight attendant position.

Commercial airlines are the busiest during the holidays and they plan on making the most revenue during these peak times. Employees are "expected to expect the unexpected." This can translate into 14 to 15 hour days, weather delays and flight cancellations, re-routing, and trips extended beyond their originally scheduled number of days.

"Quick-call" schedule changes do happen to line holders as well as reserves. Bad weather, mechanical problems, as well as crew legalities (inadequate rest times, over-flown schedules) all play a part in disrupting the airline schedule. When problems arise, they must be solved quickly in an attempt to keep the passengers content and continuing on to their destinations.

A flight departure time may need to be changed to accommodate and facilitate the smooth operation of the airline. Being prepared for such changes is mandatory. When you are on duty you must keep a reliable contact number with the company scheduling department at all times. Also, keeping someone on your crew informed of your whereabouts on an overnight is necessary. This is a safety issue as well as a scheduling one. Safety, because of the possibilities of illness or injury while on the overnight; scheduling, in case of a delay, cancellation or re-routing of your flight. Although you may be on a layover (sometimes called RON) you are still on duty. You may have already checked in for your three-day trip, flown the first day as scheduled only to receive an early call from sched-uling on the second day advising you and the crew of a mechanical or weather delay/cancellation which could affect the entire day two and day three. This is how a three-day trip can sometimes turn into a four-day trip. Flexibility is an absolute necessity for a flight attendant.

PROBATION AND RESERVE

As a new flight attendant, you will need to complete two rites of passage: probation and reserve. Each airline has its own time frame for probation but the majority of them require at least six months from the date of employment as a flight attendant.

During probation, you will be under strict and constant performance scrutiny. You will be given surprise evaluation rides, uniform checks, and constant performance/behavior critiques by your supervisors and fellow crew members. This is a very important phase of your career and vital that you maintain the professional image you were hired to present.

I found the probation period stressful because I wanted very much to perform my duties to the satisfaction of my evaluators as well as my passengers. I remember an incident that occurred on one of my check rides. I was preparing the galley for landing by stowing trays, locking latches, and trying to keep an ear keyed to the appropriate signals concerning the imminent landing. Out of the lavatory came a male passenger and he fainted right next to me! I immediately looked at my evaluator in horror. I asked, "Do you want me to take care of him?" I actually thought he was acting out a problem for my evaluation! He was for real, however, and I attended to him and he quickly regained consciousness.

Probation can be an unforgiving time because it can be the end of your career without the benefit of a second chance.

I recall a story about a new-hire who made the mistake of counting on the hotel for her early morning wake-up call.

Unfortunately, the wake-up call she received was from the captain informing her that the entire crew, and their ride to the airport, was downstairs waiting for her. Her tardiness caused the flight to depart about five minutes late and she consequently lost her job. No excuses, no second chances. I was able to learn from others to rely on no one (hotel wake-up services included) to assure that I am at work on time. Lesson: Get a good alarm clock!

Because probation is at the beginning of your career, you will most likely be on reserve at the same time (and for many months beyond).

Reserve does not at all mean you are an "extra" employee. Companies plan entire schedules with reserves in mind. A reserve flight attendant does have a monthly schedule, but instead of including specific trips with their associated check-ins, check-outs, and overnight cities, the schedule will reflect the days on call and days off.

A reserve flight attendant must be available to work during his

Sample Monthly Reserve Schedule						
Reserve Bid Block #s	4401 Thru 4403	4404 Thru 4406	4407 Thru 4408	4409 Thru 4413	4414	4415
Mon. Dec 1					OFF	
Tues, Dec 2					OFF	
Wed, Dec 3					OFF	
Thu, Dec 4					OFF	
Fri, Dec 5		OFF	OFF	OFF		OFF
Sat, Dec 6	OFF	OFF	OFF	OFF		OFF
Sun, Dec 7	OFF	OFF	OFF			OFF
Mon, Dec 8	OFF	OFF	OFF			OFF
Tue, Dec 9	OFF		OFF		OFF	OFF
Wed, Dec 10					OFF	OFF
Thu, Dec 11						OFF
Fri, Dec 12				OFF		
Sat, Dec 13		OFF		OFF		
Sun, Dec 14	OFF	OFF		OFF		
Mon, Dec 15	OFF	OFF	OFF		OFF	
Tue, Dec 16	OFF		OFF		OFF	
Wed, Dec 17					OFF	
Thu, Dec 18						OFF
Fri, Dec 19				OFF		OFF
Sat, Dec 20				OFF		
Sun, Dec 21	OFF	OFF		OFF		
Mon, Dec 22	OFF	OFF	OFF	OFF		
Tue, Dec 23			OFF	OFF	OFF	
Wed, Dec 24				OFF	OFF	
Thu, Dec 25						OFF
Fri, Dec 26						OFF
Sat. Dec 27						
Sun, Dec 28	OFF	OFF				
Mon, Dec 29	OFF	OFF	OFF			
Tue, Dec 30			OFF			

Proceeding down the column, each blank is a day that the flight attendant must be available to fly.

designated times "on call." This means you must have a phone, cell phone, or pager and be able to be reached within a designated time span. Busy signals may be tolerated for as little as 10 minutes (each airline has its own rules). Cell phones have their own unique set of problems. Call waiting is a helpful feature. A pager doesn't always work indoors, in a car, or outside of a certain range. Any time an "unable to contact" is recorded by scheduling, it could be grounds for termination or some other kind of discipline (especially while on probation).

In addition to the requirement of being able to contact you, each airline will most likely have a time or distance criterion concerning how far away from your domicile you may be while on call. This can range from as little as an hour to as much as a rather subjective "reasonable distance." Many crew members who live outside of this company-defined radius must commute to their domicile before going on call. They live in a hotel room or apartment (sometimes called a "crash pad") shared with other crew members while awaiting the call from scheduling (which may not come). The expense of these pre-work accommodations is paid for by the individual crew members.

Reserves are vital to the smooth operation of an airline. When a flight attendant must call in sick for a scheduled trip, or a weather or aircraft mechanical problem causes the crew to become "illegal" to continue with their current flight sequence, an added flight such as a charter is scheduled, or a flight attendant must be replaced for any other reason, the reserves are called in.

Each airline has its own rules and time frames pertaining to reserve. In fact, some major airlines require all flight attendants to be on reserve at some point during each year. So a flight attendant with 22 years of seniority will still have to "sit" reserve despite her years with the company. Most companies maintain that the reserve status is usually regarded as a "junior" one. However, depending on your domicile and the seniority required to hold a position there, a long time with the airline does not guarantee that you will be able to hold a regular line of flying. I can personally attest to this: I had to sit reserve when I moved from Los Angeles, a large domicile, to San Diego, a very small one, even though I had over 10 years with my airline.

The rate of growth of your airline is another factor that will determine the length of time you will spend on reserve. I was very fortunate when

I was hired. It was a time of active hiring and airline deregulation. I spent only three months on reserve before I was able to hold a line. This is very unusual. I suggest you attempt to determine the current or future growth status of the airline you select to interview with. Talk to current flight attendants and other employees about how long you might expect to be on reserve. Sometimes you can learn about the growth of an airline by reading the business section of major newspapers.

Reserve and probation are different for every company. What seems to be a constant, though, is that the lifestyle is hectic and uncertain. Once again, flexibility is the key to enjoying this exciting career.

BENEFITS

What is usually one of the first thoughts you have when thinking about a career as an airline employee? "Flying for free all around the world!?"

Many flight attendants select their company, not based upon wages or domiciles, but upon the destinations the airline serves that would also be great vacation spots. Flight benefits for the employee, spouse, children, and parents have always been an incredibly desirable perk of the industry. Add to this the bonus of hotels and cruise companies offering discounts of up to 50% and this is a golden benefit to the employee who enjoys traveling. The airlines are well aware of the importance of these benefits to employees and have continued to offer them with little or no changes. Reduced rate travel will continue to be a high priority benefit for all airline employees.

In order to enjoy these non-revenue travel benefits, you will need adequate days off — in other words — vacation. Vacation is earned according to the number of full months of employment in the preceding calendar year. Most major airlines are consistent on this issue. Airlines have their own formulas by which they add and subtract vacation days. However, unlike the way most non-airline companies calculate vacation, your vacation will be calculated in hours and is paid at your hourly rate. Some airlines will pay for the value of any trips that must be dropped if they are scheduled during your vacation. In other words, if you have a four-day trip that has its last day scheduled on the first day of your vacation, the entire trip will be dropped and you will be paid for it.

You could significantly extend your vacation by bidding trips which lead into and out of your vacation, thus ensuring more days off than your basic vacation days (you could turn a seven-day vacation into 14 days).

Other airlines pay a specific hourly rate per day of vacation and do not pay for trips missed. Additionally, an airline may pay a lower rate per day if you take your vacation in less than seven-day increments. This is to make it undesirable for you to spread your vacation days thinly throughout the year. As you can see, creative bidding can help maximize your vacation.

Medical, dental, eye care, and prescription insurance is offered to employees by just about every regional and major airline. Airlines have their own coverage packages that they present to the employee for selection. Most airlines require a monthly premium (via payroll deduction). Gone, in most cases, is the 100% coverage of the past. Insurance coverage is usually available to all employees and their families.

Other benefits are often available from the airlines, such as company-paid life insurance, optional employee-paid life insurance, 401(k), and regular retirement plans.

DOMICILES AND LIVING ARRANGEMENTS

Potential flight attendants are asked during their first group interview if they would be willing to relocate to other cities (domiciles) as a condition of employment. Of course "yes" is the appropriate answer. When it comes time for the actual move, however, many people are reluctant and intimidated by the prospect.

Most major airline companies will provide for living arrangements only while in initial training.

It is during training that you will be asked to compile your domicile "wish list." You must list which of the airline's domiciles you would like to be assigned from most to least desirable. Multiple choices are necessary as your first or second (or third, or fourth) choice may not have an opening at the time of assignment.

During your initial training, friendships will be made and roommates will be found. The domicile you are awarded will determine how many roommates will be needed to pay the rent. "Crash pad" is the term most often attributed to the new-hire living conditions, although this term and condition may exist throughout your career should you decide not to live close enough to your domicile to utilize ground transportation. Living in New York City with the high cost of living and receiving a new-hire salary doesn't allow for a Central Park locale with only one roommate. It sometimes requires six or more just to meet the rent. Remember, you won't all be there at the same time, but trusting others and sharing bathrooms, telephones and possibly even beds, may be necessary and can create problems for even the most sociable of the group. These living arrangements are usually short-lived. Being able to cope with the crash pad lifestyle is often a necessary step to succeed as a flight attendant.

Note

Chapter 4

Could this Be Your Employer?

Picking up and filling out an application for employment is often the only research conducted by a flight attendant hopeful. However, in order to increase your chances of success, you must be aware of what an airline expects of its new-hire flight attendants.

This chapter will provide you with a broad overview of the flight attendant interviewing process, training expectations, benefits, pay, etc. Knowing what to expect from the airlines, and understanding what is expected of you, will help make your interviews and your initial flight attendant training less stressful.

You will notice that some listings are more complete than others, this is because the information was provided directly from the individual airlines. Remember, this is not a complete list of the airlines you may want to pursue. If we have not listed the address of an airline you are interested in, call the airline's main reservations number and ask for the airline's company headquarters address. Also, always ask if the airline has an "employment opportunities" hotline.

Airlines list upcoming Flight Attendant Open Houses under the Employment/Help Wanted sections of local newspapers. Normally the Open Houses are conducted in larger cities. If you live in a small town it would be a good idea to regularly review a newspaper from a large city close to you.

   As you read through this chapter keep in mind these important facts that are fairly consistent within the airline industry.

   • You will notice that pay is determined by FLIGHT TIME. You may see a listing that states a flight attendant is guaranteed pay for a 70-hour month, keep in mind this is flight time only. For example, although you may actually be on duty from 5am to 1:30pm (eight and a half hours) your actual flight time may only be five hours. An example of this type of trip would be: Your check-in is at 5am. You leave Denver at 6am (MST) and work a trip to Chicago. You arrive in Chicago at 9:30am (CST). This equals 2 1/2 hours of flight time. Then you must wait in Chicago for 2 1/2 hours for your return trip to Denver. You leave Chicago at Noon (CST) and land in Denver at 1:30pm (MST). You receive another 2 1/2 hours of flight time.

   • Per-diem (expense money) is usually paid for each hour on duty. This means from check-in to completing your trip back at your domicile. Per-diem can run anywhere from $1.00 an hour to $1.95 an hour depending on the airline.

   • You do not normally receive a salary during initial flight attendant training. However, many airlines do provide room and board during the training period.

   • The first set of uniforms, including luggage, is paid for by the new employee. Most new-hires choose to pay for the uniforms through payroll deduction. Payroll deductions can be minimal.

   • Flight crew hotel and ground transportation on layovers is arranged and paid for by the airline.

For information and/or applications:

   Alaska Airlines, Inc.
   Human Resources
   Box 68900, Seattle, WA 98168

   American Airlines
   Flight Attendant Recruitment
   PO Box 650071, Dallas, TX 75265-0071

American Eagle, Inc.
Flight Attendant Recruitment
PO Box 619415, Dallas-Fort Worth Airport, TX 75261

America West Airlines, Inc.
Inflight Service
4000 E. Sky Harbor Blvd., Phoenix, AZ 85034

Continental Airlines, Inc.
Inflight Training
4375 Wright Road, Houston, TX 77032

Delta Air Lines, Inc.
System Employment Manager
General Offices
Hartsfield Atlanta International Airport, Atlanta, GA 30320

Northwest Airlines
Flight Attendant Human Resources
MSF1470
Northwest Drive, St. Paul, MN 55111-3034

Southwest Airlines
Inflight Services
Box 36611, Love Field, Dallas, TX 75235

TWA
Employment Office
PO Box 20126, Kansas City, MO 64195

United Airlines
PO Box 66100, Chicago, Illinois 60666

USAirways, Inc.
Inflight Services
2345 Crystal Drive, Crystal Park 4, Arlington, VA 22227

AMERICAN AIRLINES
Domiciles:

Boston, New York City, Washington DC, Miami, Chicago, Dallas-Fort Worth, Puerto Rico, Los Angeles, San Francisco. International domiciles are Raleigh-Durham (NC), and Seattle.

Interview Process:

American Airlines no longer conducts "open house" type interviews. They now require an initial computer-conducted telephone screening system that allows the applicant to pre-interview by answering several questions. The answers allow American Airlines to determine if the caller is employee material. If the caller meets the necessary requirements, an application will then be mailed to the prospective employee.

If American is hiring, the applicant can expect the following to take place at the initial appointment:

1. A briefing where airline representatives introduce the company to the applicants.
2. A group interview. There may be up to 25 applicants per group. All are given an opportunity to answer and ask questions of an American recruiter.
3. A one-on-one interview with a recruiter.

Educational Requirements:

High school/GED and two years post-high school experience are required. A college degree is not required. It has been noted that college graduates do not necessarily perform better during training or in the aircraft. American does look for prospective employees with face-to-face past customer service experience.

Language Requirements:

American is actively seeking foreign language skills in Spanish, French, Japanese, German, Dutch, Swedish, and Portuguese. Fluency in any of these languages is a tremendous plus.

Other Requirements:

Age: American encourages all ages to apply for employment starting at 20 years old. American has been a front-runner in the current practice of hiring applicants who are over 40 years of age. Many of their flight attendants have over 30 years of seniority.

Height: Although American no longer has a height minimum, a maximum height of six feet is still in effect.

Weight: Weight maximums are no longer enforced. However, employees are expected to maintain a healthy height-to-weight ratio.

Training Site:

Fort Worth, Texas.

Training:

American Airlines conducts a six-weeks-and-four-days unpaid initial training course. Room and board are provided by the company. By the third week of training each new-hire will receive a domicile assignment.

Pay:

After the completion of training, pay and benefits begin. Approximate salary for a new-hire reserve flying a 71-75 flight time month is $1297.00. An hourly per diem is paid while away from domicile on a trip.

Uniforms:

Flight attendants purchase their first uniforms and luggage for approximately $600-$800. Payroll deduction is available for this expense.

Union:

American Airlines is affiliated with the Association of Professional Flight Attendants (APFA). American is a "closed shop" that requires the entire flight attendant population to be members. Currently, the dues are $35.00 per month and are paid via payroll deduction.

Benefits:

A 401(k) program is available. It is composed of self-contributed, unmatched funds. Profit sharing is currently in effect at American. The proceeds may be deferred to the 401(k) plan. A choice of major medical and dental insurance coverage is provided with a portion of the premium paid by the employee via payroll deduction. Flight attendant retirement program is available. Pass benefits are available to employees after the six-month probation has been completed. Spouses, dependent children, and parents are extended identical travel benefits.

Common Mistakes:

These were mentioned as specifically occurring during American Airlines interviews:

- Bringing a water bottle into the interview.
- Having a pager or cell phone ring during the interview.
- Being late to the interview.
- Not being prepared.
- Having a conflicting appointment scheduled too closely together.
- Asking how long the interview is going to last.

Interesting Facts:

American Airlines is planning an internet website in the near future.

AMERICAN EAGLE

Domiciles:

New York City, Miami, Dallas-Fort Worth, Chicago, Los Angeles, Puerto Rico. Preferred choices not always available. Relocation between domiciles is at employee's expense.

Interview Process:

American Eagle requires that an application be requested through the mail. After a request is received, an application will be mailed.

When American Eagle is conducting interviews, the following can be expected:

1. The completion of additional paperwork.
2. A briefing by the head of Flight Attendant recruiting, followed by a video introducing the airline.
3. A group interview with approximately six applicants.
4. An individual interview.

The entire process will be completed in one day. By the end of this interview process an applicant will either be offered employment or thanked for their interest in American Eagle and excused. A 10-year background check will be conducted on each applicant offered the opportunity of employment.

It is suggested that the applicant bring the following to the interview:
- Personality.
- Enthusiasm.
- Energy.
- Confidence.
- A knowledge of the airline.
- Customer service skills.

Educational Requirements:

High school graduation or equivalent.

Other Requirements:

Minimum requirements are as follows:
- Minimum age - 19 years old.
- Customer service experience.
- Photo identification.
- Have a legal right to work in the United States.
- Ability to work nights, shifts, weekends, and holidays.
- Willingness to relocate.
- Willingness to work multiple day trips.
- No visible tattoos.
- Height between 5 feet and 5 feet-10 inches.
- Possess passport or original birth certificate.

Training Site:

Space available transportation is provided on American Airlines or American Eagle from any city served to the training site in Dallas-Ft. Worth, Texas.

Training:

Training is completed through a 3 1/2 week course. American Eagle does not pay any salary during training. Training includes: classroom, homework, and training flights. Written and practical test scores, in accordance with American Eagle and FAA requirements, must be 90% or higher. The course schedule is fairly intense, lasting from 8am until 5pm Monday through Friday with an occasional day lasting as late as 8pm. Weekends are also scheduled when deemed necessary.
Attendance during the entire course (including all functions) is mandatory.

The most difficult segments of training appear to be the safety drills with first aid being a close second. The ability to memorize is a big plus during training.

Pay:

Due to the fact that the regional airlines have a lower pay scale than the majors, a desire for the benefits is often the motivation for employment. For the first six months, the pay is $11.33 per flight hour with a 70-hour monthly guarantee. Additionally, $1.00 is paid for every hour on duty (per diem) while on trips. The pay rate rises incrementally with the highest rate of $18.54 being attained at the 10-year seniority level. These pay rates are competitive with most other regional airlines (i.e., United Express, USAirways Express, Skywest, etc.).

Uniforms:

Flight attendants are required to purchase the initial set of uniforms at a cost of approximately $750. Payroll deduction over a two-year period is available.

Union:

The AFA (Association of Flight Attendants) is the representative of American Eagle flight attendants.

Benefits:

After the 6-month probationary period, flight attendants are eligible for unlimited standby travel on American Eagle and American Airlines. Family members are included in travel benefits. These are extended to spouses and dependent children up to a specified age. Additionally, each employee is entitled to an annual allowance of 16 one-way, taxable service-charge passes for use by relatives and friends.

As a regional affiliate of American Airlines, American Eagle flight attendants enjoy the security of stable employment with competitive medical and dental benefits. The company will match employee contributions to a 401(k) account. Travel throughout the American Airlines and American Eagle worldwide system is a definite plus.

Common Mistakes:
- Arriving at the interview unprepared.
- Guarded or dishonest responses.
- Inability of applicants to think on their feet.

Interesting Facts:
- Since American Eagle operates a fleet of aircraft with a seating capacity of 34-64, it is essential that flight attendants are comfortable working alone. Leaders verses followers are sought. Independent, self-confident individuals will excel with American Eagle.
- The most senior flight attendant has 16 years with the company.
- Insurance is not provided during training. Maintain your own coverage until completion of course.
- If requested by training personnel, you must agree to a change of style or color of hair or makeup.
- Working for American Eagle is often a stepping-stone for flight attendants who will leave for a major airline.
- Traits American Eagle finds important for their flight attendants are:
  - Dependability.
  - Attention to detail.
  - Ability to speak clearly.
  - A sense of humor.
  - Customer service experience.
- A typical class age profile is as follows: 19-20 - 14%, 21-29 - 58%, 30-39 - 14%, 40-49 - 9%, 50-59 - 4%, 60+ - 1%.

USAIRWAYS

Domiciles:
Baltimore, Boston, Philadelphia, Pittsburgh, Washington, DC, Charlotte (NC). Initial base assignments are offered to fill existing vacancies. A request for a transfer will be honored as vacancies occur.

Interview Process:
USAirways interviews 100 applicants for every three flight attendants

hired. Announcement of an Open House is often published in local newspapers. If searching for second-language applicants, a notation will appear in the same advertisement. The 800 reservation number may be called to inquire about obtaining an application. When attending an Open House, applications will be provided and time will be allotted for its completion. A group interview will then be conducted. It consists of 25 to 30 applicants. An overview of the company will be presented with the opportunity to ask questions and speak in a group setting. If successful at the group interview, a second interview with two employee representatives will be arranged. There are a total of three interviews the applicant must successfully complete.

Educational Requirements:
Must possess a high school diploma or GED.

Language Requirements:
USAirways does not require a foreign language. Occasionally need will arise for hiring employees with second language abilities.

Other Requirements:
- Must be 21 years of age or older.
- Must be willing to relocate to any of USAirways crew domiciles.
- Must maintain a passport and foreign visa if applicable.
- USAirways does not have weight or height guidelines. Candidates must be able to demonstrate the ability to operate and reach all safety equipment and be able to move comfortably throughout the aircraft.
- Vision must be correctable to 20/30.

Training Site:
Pittsburgh, Pennsylvania.

Training:
Initial flight attendant training is an extensive five-week course with classroom and "hands on" training. Aircraft mock-ups are used for simulation of emergencies such as preparing the cabin for evacuation and fire-fighting. Also covered in class are Federal Aviation Regulations, aircraft types, safety and first aid procedures, cabin service procedures,

airline terminology, uniform standards and grooming techniques. Written exams must be passed with a FAA-mandated passing score of 85-90% minimum. Out of town trainees will be provided with living arrangements during training.

Pay:

A flight attendant's salary is based upon the number of hours flown each month. Monthly hours range from 71 to 105 hours. The following information is based on the minimum salary for a 71-hour flight month: First year - $18.32 per hour ($1300.72 per month), fourteenth year (maximum pay rate) - $39.44 per hour ($2800.24 per month). Additionally, for each hour away from domicile on a trip, $1.90 is paid for per diem.

Uniforms:

After graduating, flight attendants are required to purchase their initial uniform items. Any subsequent changes to the uniform will be paid for by the company. Replacement items are also provided for by USAirways.

Union:

The Association of Flight Attendants (AFA) represents the USAirways flight attendant group. Dues are $35.00 a month and paid via payroll deduction.

Benefits:

All USAirways employees receive a comprehensive benefit package including: health care, dental care, life insurance, company paid vacation and sick leave, disability and retirement benefits, participation in the Employee Stock Ownership Program (ESOP), 401(k), educational assistance, and maternity leaves of absence. Space available travel privileges for employees and family on USAirways and USAirways Express are available for an annual fee. A limited number of space available round-trip passes for friends and ineligible family members are available each year at a reduced rate. Passes become available when the six-month probation period is completed.

Common Mistakes:

- Many people fail to complete the entire application form.

Interesting Facts:

- Past customer service is a definite plus for interviewing.
- A background check will be performed to verify past employment. More than a 60-day lapse without employment will require a reference who can account for that period of time.
- A verification check will be made to confirm the highest level of education attained.
- Become knowledgeable about the position of flight attendant. This will relay the appearance that you are truly motivated towards this career.

UNITED AIRLINES

Domiciles:

Boston, Chicago, Denver, Honolulu, Las Vegas, Los Angeles, Miami, Newark, New York City, Philadelphia, San Francisco, Seattle, Washington, D.C. International Domiciles: Frankfort, London, Hong Kong, Paris, Santiago, Taipei, Tokyo.

Interview Process:

United will not accept applications through the mail. In order to be considered, all applicants must attend an Open House (at the expense of the applicant). Open Houses are conducted in major cities within the United States. Applicants can expect the following to occur during the Open House interview:

1. Complete a written application.
2. Stand and talk about yourself in front of the entire group of applicants for 1-2 minutes.
3. Take a short written exam. This exam is designed to provide the airline with insight into the applicant's probable success in the flight attendant training program.

Interviewers critique an applicant's personal appearance (makeup, clothing); body language (good eye contact, smiling, strong speaking voice); ability to communicate (good eye contact, smiling, strong speaking voice); dependability (being on time). The applicant is asked to sign a waiver allowing past employers to discuss dependability, quality of work, and overall work performance.

If you do not interview well, you will not be passed on to the second interview. It is extremely important to learn how to present yourself to a large group of people.

If the applicant is successful in impressing the recruiting team, the next step is a Final Interview Phase. This lasts three to four hours and includes:

Video Test: This test is composed of hypothetical situations presented on video. Several times during the video the tape stops, questions are asked, and the applicant must choose from several possible answers.

Group Exercise: Applicants are grouped together and must solve a problem. Recruiters are looking for those applicants that show an ability to work well with others and appear to have strong problem solving skills. They also weed out those applicants who are too aggressive or too quiet.

One-On-One Interview: A personal interview with a flight attendant interviewer.

United Airlines is looking for applicants who meet the following criteria: strong customer service skills; sensitive to the needs of others; dependable; good communicator; flexible; second language skills.

Educational Requirements:

A high school or equivalent is required. Customer service experience is a definite plus.

Language Requirements:

United actively seeks candidates with at least one foreign language in addition to English. Preferred languages are those spoken in Asia, Latin America and Europe. A demonstration of language proficiency may be required during the interview process.

Other Requirements:

- Applicants must be at least 19 years old.
- There is no minimum height requirement; however, applicants

cannot be over six feet tall (some of the galleys on the airplanes are six feet high). All applicants must be able to reach 82 inches vertically (the height of the overhead bins).
- A healthy height-to-weight ratio is expected.
- Vision must be correctable to 20/30 with contacts or glasses.
- Each applicant must be a U.S. citizen or an alien with the legal right to accept employment in the United States.
- Prior to training a complete physical examination is required.

Training Site:
Chicago, Illinois.

Training:
A seven-week, tuition-free training program with free room and board is provided. Training is conducted on the weekends and in the evenings. There is required homework.

The areas covered include training on all United airplanes, food and beverage service, emergency procedures, first aid, and city codes. There are written and oral examinations.

Pay:
Flight attendants are paid upon the number of hours flown per month. Reserve flight attendants are guaranteed 75 hours per month at $19.06 per hour. Per diem is paid for each hour away from domicile.

Uniforms:
New hire flight attendants must pay for their first uniforms. The cost is approximately $700.00 for both luggage and uniform. Payroll deduction is available.

Union:
The Association of Flight Attendants (AFA) represents the flight attendant group. Dues are $39.00 a month and may be paid through payroll deduction.

Benefits:
United Airlines offers an employee stock purchase plan, 401(k), and has its own credit union. The airline also offers an extensive package of medical and dental insurance, life insurance, pension plan, and paid vacations. Medical and dental is extended to the employee's spouse and dependent children. The employee, spouse, and dependent children are eligible for unlimited travel benefits after the employee's six-month probation period is completed.

Interesting Facts:
- Background checks are performed on each applicant.
- A profile of the flight attendants hired at United Airlines in a recent one-year period looked like this:
  - 80% were 25 or older.
  - 46% were over 30 years old. United hired 51 flight attendants over the age of 50. Two new hires were over 60.
  - 88% had at least one year of college.
  - 49% had an Associates or Bachelor's degree.

TRANS WORLD AIRLINES (TWA)
Domiciles:
Main Bases: New York City, St. Louis, Missouri. Satellite Bases: Los Angeles, San Francisco, Kansas City, Atlanta, Washington, DC, Chicago, Boston.

Interview Process:
Applicants are screened by TWA personnel in a group session. Applicants must be prepared to show they are physically able to perform the duties of a flight attendant. A drug screening and ten-year background verification will be required.

Educational Requirements:
High School Diploma.

Language Requirements:
TWA requires fluency in the English language. A second language is desired, however, not required.

Other Requirements:

- Be at least 20 years of age.
- Be between 5'2" and 6'2" in height. Weight must be in proportion to height.
- Must be a current U.S. citizen or be authorized to work in the United States. You must be able to obtain a valid passport and a French visa. You must not be restricted from obtaining visas to other countries. You must be able to enter and leave all countries served by TWA. Individuals with non-US passports must assume all responsibility for visa requirements as they pertain to their individual passports.
- Must have two years of public contact experience.
- Corrected vision must be 20/50 or better in each eye.
- Uncorrected vision cannot exceed 20/200.
- Must be willing to accept relocation.

Training Site:
St. Louis, Missouri.

Training:
The training course lasts six weeks and is conducted by TWA Inflight Services.

Pay & Benefits:
Not available.

Uniforms:
TWA requires their new hires to purchase the flight attendant uniform.

Union:
TWA flight attendants are affiliated with the International Association of Machinists (IAM).

Interesting Facts:
Applicants not meeting the minimum qualifications at the time of the interview may reapply in six months.

Chapter 5

Making Yourself A More Marketable Applicant

When I first became interested in becoming a flight attendant there were advertisements in the back of magazines promising placement with an airline if you attended their flight attendant training programs. These were, in my opinion, empty, money-making ploys designed for that purpose rather than the training and placement of flight attendants. Also, many junior colleges offered "stewardess" courses for college credit. My reply to anyone asking about these courses has been to suggest applicants focus on getting customer service experience instead.

The airlines train their flight attendants according to FAA requirements and the airline's specifications regardless of previous training elsewhere. Airlines would prefer to see potential flight attendants have customer service experience rather than classroom time. Previous customer service experience is a valuable tool for helping you ease into your new career smoothly.

CUSTOMER SERVICE EXPERIENCE

Whenever you are on duty as a flight attendant, you are involved in some type of customer service: Meeting people, helping them with their baggage, solving their seating and connection problems, offering food and drinks, assisting a passenger who is ill, etc.

In order to prove to the interviewer that you are skilled in customer service, you must gain some direct customer service experience.

There are many jobs available that can give you this experience. Here are some good choices:

- Waitressing
- Bartending
- Hotel Front Desk Clerk
- Hotel Concierge
- Retail Sales Clerk
- Receptionist for a professional office (medical, dental, legal, accounting, etc.)
- Tour Guide
- Camp Counselor
- Lifeguard

Perhaps you have never held a job that required direct customer contact, and your current job does not entail working with people. You still need the experience — so what do you do?

Look to volunteer work. There are many opportunities within volunteer organizations that can offer you customer service experience. Some organizations which may offer opportunities to work with people include:

- Speakers Bureaus within any volunteer organization
- Hospital Volunteer
- Nursing Home Volunteer
- Coaching athletics for youth organizations or within scouting
- Docent programs (tour guides) at the local zoo
- Tour Guide at local museums

Do not take your volunteer responsibilities lightly. You need to take your commitment to the organization seriously. It is not enough simply to join a group and not do any of the work!

Every organization needs volunteers. You only need to pick up the phone book and start making calls; someone out there will be happy for your help. Make sure you pick an area you enjoy. Volunteering is an excellent way to gain, and hone, your customer service skills while, at the same time, contributing to your community.

OTHER HELPFUL SKILLS:

Second Language Skills: A second language is not a requirement for employment for the majority of the commercial airlines. Some, of course, do require fluency in a language other than English, especially if the airline is a foreign carrier or one that has international flights. If you are capable of speaking and understanding a second language, it will be a benefit to you and the company that hires you. Although it isn't necessary to run out and sign up for classes in another language, it could prove to be a tremendous asset when interviewing.

CPR And First Aid: You don't need to be certified in CPR before you apply to the airline. First aid, with CPR training, is covered during initial airline training and then every year during recurrent training. However, having your certification before you apply will show a responsible motivation on your part. Although airlines no longer require flight attendants to be nurses you must be comfortable with handling a bloody or potentially life threatening situation by yourself. This type of situation very possibly will happen in the course of your career. Are you up to the task? If you know ahead of time that the answer is "No," another position with an airline should be considered.

OVERVIEW

Today's flight attendant delivers a high standard of professionalism. Meeting that standard takes commitment and dedication. If, after your interview, you feel good about how you fared, chances are the interviewers will have received your "positive message" as well. If, on the other hand, you don't feel as if you were able to present the best impression, work on those areas you feel need refining. Reapply in a few months with improved skills. Many current flight attendants were not hired on their first, second, or even third try. If this is truly the career you desire, continue to work toward achieving your goal. The result is well worth all your time and effort.

Notes

Chapter 6

A Successful Interview

STEP 1: INFORMATION COLLECTING, APPLICATIONS, COVER LETTERS, RESUME, LETTERS OF RECOMMENDATION.

At some time during the fight attendant interviewing process you will have to fill out an employment application, or provide a resume. Whatever documentation you are asked to provide it will make your life a lot easier if you have all the information you need prior to sitting down and completing the application.

Another positive reason for gathering this information early is that it will also allow you to solve any problems or correct any mistakes you discover along the way. Problems can range from an employer listing the wrong employment dates to discovering that your college has no record of you!

You may not necessarily need all this information. But it is better to have it and not need it than to be asked for it and not be able to provide it.

INFORMATION COLLECTING WORKSHEET

Research and write down all the following information. Organize it on paper and use this information to help you fill out applications at home. Always take this information with you to flight attendant open houses to use in filling out on-the-spot applications.

WORK HISTORY

List your work history beginning with most recent and ending with high school jobs.

- List dates of your employment,
- Salary,
- Company name, address, phone number, and supervisors name,
- Job title and duties,
- Any awards or honors you received through your employment,
- Reason for leaving.

If you truly cannot find an address or phone number for a past employer, you may still be asked to present some kind of documentation that you were employed. Collect: W-2s, employee critiques, or a notarized letter from a former co-worker stating that you worked there.

If your reason for leaving is "termination" think carefully about what words you want to use to describe the situation. If it won't make things worse, you might want to call your past employer and ask what will be said about your departure. If you have a job termination in your background, it will be very important to acquire a positive letter of recommendation from an employer you had AFTER the job where you were terminated. This positive letter will help show that you have solved whatever problems you had that resulted in the termination.

If you have more than two months between jobs when you were not in school, list what you were doing. For example: *6/97 to 9/97: Actively seeking employment.*

EDUCATION

List all your education in reverse chronological order. If you have a college degree you need not list your high school education.

Example: *B.A. in Psychology, University of New Hampshire, Dover, New Hampshire.*

List all education awards or achievements.

Example: *Graduated with a Grade Point Average of 3.7 (on a 4.0 scale)* or *Secretary/Treasurer of Student Body.* If you paid for your own education make sure you list this also!

Do not list the DATES of your graduation. Companies are very concerned about age discrimination and do not want any information that would possibly show your age.

SPECIALIZED TRAINING

List any specialized training you may have.

Example: *Completed Berlitz course in Spanish,* or *CPR course through YWCA.*

COMMUNITY INVOLVEMENT

List any past or present volunteer experience.

Example: *Volunteer for American Red Cross. On-call for local disaster relief (1997 to present).*

INTERESTS OR HOBBIES

List specific interests or hobbies.

Example: Don't list *"reading"* as a hobby. List as *"Enjoy reading historical novels."*

ADDITIONAL

Collect letters of reference from as many employers as possible. Make sure all past employers know they may be called for employment verification.

Gather letters of recommendation from PERSONAL references.

Get correct addresses and phone numbers for all personal and employer references.

APPLICATIONS

Although the process of obtaining an application may vary, most major and regional airlines will mail an application at your request (be sure to enclose a self-addressed, stamped #10 envelope for the airline to send the application back to you). Applications may also be available from the airline ticket counter at the airport.

You, not a friend, should pick up the application as this will give you the opportunity to observe the company employees in action. After watching them, are you still interested in becoming a fellow employee? Or, would you rather move to the next airline's ticket counter and try there?

Large airlines usually have one application that is used for many positions in the company. You must list the specific job you are seeking. Don't be surprised if you are asked if another position, such as ticket agent, would be acceptable. (Of course, as you're reading this book, it's safe to assume you are most interested in becoming a flight attendant. However, you may miss out on an employment opportunity with the company you've selected by being inflexible. Many flight attendants are intra-company transfers from other departments. This is definitely something to consider because when you apply, the airline you want to work for may not be hiring flight attendants.)

While filling out the application, I cannot stress enough the need for attention to detail. Follow directions and read everything twice before filling out the final paperwork. Make a rough draft first. Once you are comfortable with your answers, type the application. (Unless the directions specifically state to PRINT the application. In that case you must fill out the application yourself.) Typing gives your application a professional edge over one that is handwritten. Proofread, especially if someone has helped you with the typing. Only you know how you intended to answer each and every question.

Filling in all the blanks and answering all the questions is extremely important. Just because you've left something blank does not make it go away. Don't leave the "Reason for Leaving" question on the application blank, even if you were fired. If you think the airline won't find out — you're wrong! Background checks are performed by every airline. Don't waste the interviewer's time, or yours, by handing in an incomplete application.

If applying for more than one airline at a time, don't forget whose application you are filling out. Pay close attention to detail. Keep your answers truthful. Do not answer "yes" to the question "Are you fluent in a foreign language?" just because you know "a little." If you realize that you don't meet the company's requirements for the position, either take action to attain what you lack or consider another career.

Photocopy your completed applications in case of loss or misplacement by the company (which sometimes happens). Always keep copies of all correspondence for your files. Additionally, review your answers prior to appearing for the interview as you may be asked to explain or expound upon your responses, and there may have been a considerable time period between when you submitted your application and the interview.

COVER LETTERS

A cover letter is not usually a requirement for the application process. However, it certainly couldn't hurt to include one (UNLESS THE DIRECTIONS SPECIFICALLY TELL YOU NOT TO SEND A COVER LETTER!). Take advantage of this opportunity to personalize yourself and your achievements for the interviewer. Include any information about yourself that you feel would be a positive addition to what has already been asked on the application. The cover letter will be read by each and every person handling the applications. It would be a benefit to you if you could find out, by calling or through an employee, the name of the person to whom you should address the cover letter. This is a further indication that you have spent some time researching the company. Keep the letter as brief as possible.

Writing Your Cover Letters

- Make sure your cover letter is on the same color/weight of paper and with the same letterhead logo as your resume.
- Use a white or ivory colored paper.
- Your cover letter should be no more than one page long.
- Each cover letter should be personalized to the specific airline.

Here is a basic format to follow when writing your cover letters:

Beginning Statement: In two to three sentences explain why you are writing.

I would like to be considered for a flight attendant position with SkyHigh Airlines. Enclosed please find my application and resume for your review.

Middle Statement: Describe the specific skills you will bring to this position in two to four sentences.

I have recently graduated from the University of Colorado with my B.A. in Psychology. During college I worked part-time in retail clothing sales and as a waitress to pay for my tuition and living expenses.

Ending Statement: Thank them and ask for an interview in one or two sentences.

After reviewing my application I hope I will be invited for an interview.

Closing: Choose a short, unobtrusive closing. "Sincerely" is safe and professional.

RESUME PREPARATION (example follows)

Some airlines ask for a resume and sometimes you are specifically told NOT to send one. However, to be on the safe side you should have a current one. If an airline requests one it can add extra information about you that may not be covered on the application. Watch out for gaps in your resume. An astute interviewer will ask about any lapse in employment. If you include a resume covering a period from 1993 through 1998 and leave out anything concerning your activity from 1994 to 1995, you most surely will be questioned about that period. If you were a student, traveled the world, or were "between jobs," say so! Just be sure you include each year's activity and/or employment. This is also an appropriate place to list your schooling and involvement in community services.

If an airline does not give directions about including a resume, you may go ahead and put one in with your application.

Resume Hints

- Keep your resume to one page.
- Personalize your objective for each airline. *Flight Attendant position with SkyHigh Airlines.*
- Use a 25lb., 100% cotton, white or ivory colored paper. Use the same paper as your cover letter.
- Do not use any airplane pictures or other "cute" logos on your resume. You want to be viewed as a professional.
- Do not list references on your resume.
- Keep the font styles simple. Do not use any more than two font styles.
- Always include on your resume: Objective, Work History, Education, Community Involvement. Always inform them you are WILLING TO RELOCATE.

PAIGE ADAMS
2345 East Avenue, #455
Denver, Colorado 80334
(303) 555-5555

OBJECTIVE
Flight Attendant for SkyHigh Airlines

WORK HISTORY
SALES ASSOCIATE / ASSISTANT MANAGER - January 1997 to present.
Quality Department Stores, Denver, Colorado.
Began as Sales Associate in the cosmetics department.
In June of 1997 was promoted to Assistant Department Manager for
Cosmetics.
Responsibilities include:
- Maintain regular schedule as a sales associate assisting customers.
- Assist sales associates with problems (customer complaints, cash
  register problems, special orders).
- Input monthly inventory numbers for all lines of cosmetics.
- Assist Department Manager with bi-yearly ordering of all cosmetic
  lines.

WAITRESS / HOST - September 1993 to December 1996.
Tyrells Grill, Denver, Colorado.
- Scheduled as a waitress or host depending on staffing needs.
- Trained new waitresses and hosts.
- Worked part-time during school year (September to June).
- Worked full-time during summers and Christmas vacations.

EDUCATION
- B.A. in Psychology/Social Studies from University of Colorado,
  Boulder, Colorado.
- Graduated with a 3.4 GPA (4.0 scale).
- Paid for all living expenses and 1/2 of tuition.

INTERESTS
- Member of Women's Doubles Tennis Team (1994-1996).
- Enjoy reading mysteries and biographies.
- Raise tomatoes and petunias.

WILLING TO RELOCATE. REFERENCES FURNISHED UPON REQUEST.

PERSONAL AND EMPLOYER LETTERS OF RECOMMENDATION
Personal

If you are fortunate enough to know someone connected with the airline you wish to apply to, by all means ask if they would be willing to write a letter of recommendation. A letter of recommendation is not necessary, but one from a respected current or past employee could be extremely helpful in getting you a second look. I must point out, though, that it is vital to your future employment that you know a few important facts about the person who is writing on your behalf. Is he or she well-respected at home, in the neighborhood, in the community? If not, it is very unlikely he or she will be held in high regard in the workplace. In fact, such a letter on your behalf could be the "kiss of death" for you. Your intuition is very important on this issue. The purpose of the letter is to enhance your application and possibility of employment, not hinder it.

The letter should describe you as someone who would be a real asset to the company.

Employer

You should also ask for a letter of recommendation each time you leave an employer. Although the airlines will contact your past employers to assure that your employment record is complete, it can't hurt to have letters on hand.

Do not send any employer letters with an application. Take them with you to the interview and offer them when the opportunity presents itself. (If you are asked a question such as "How would your past employers describe you?," you would answer the question and then say something like, "I have a letter from my current employer with me. Would you care to see it?" If they say "no" don't push it.)

STEP 2: FLIGHT ATTENDANT SELF-EVALUATION WORKSHEET

In any interview it is the applicant's responsibility to share information with the interviewer. It is NOT the interviewer's responsibility to drag information out of you. It is imperative that you learn to become a good "information giver."

That's nice, you are thinking, but how do I do that?

It is quite straightforward. You must provide specific examples that clearly show HOW you handle yourself in various situations, and WHY you would be a good candidate for the flight attendant position.

No matter what type of question you are asked, whether it be a question concerning your background (what did you do when...?) or a situational question (what would you do if...?) you must answer in specifics!

Let's look at two different approaches to answering the same question. As you will notice, these two applicants ARE SAYING THE SAME THING—however one is general and one is specific.

An applicant is asked, "Why do you want to be a flight attendant?"
The unprepared applicant (general answer) would say:
"I like people, and I love to travel."
The prepared applicant (specific answer) would answer:
"I was a waitress for three years while at the same time working part-time in retail sales. I chose these jobs because I really enjoy working with people. In addition, for one week every year I take part of my savings and visit a different part of the country. The most important reason I want to be a flight attendant is because I truly love meeting new people, problem solving, and helping out. To be traveling while working with people is just an added bonus!"

Do you see the difference? Put yourself in the INTERVIEWER'S shoes: Whom would you hire? Of these two responses which one makes you feel as if the applicant truly understands and desires a flight attendant career?

In order to provide specific answers you must do some self-evaluation prior to your interviews. Take the time to critique what skills you possess and what responsibilities you will encounter on a daily basis as a flight attendant. Then review your past experiences to uncover situations where you fulfilled these same types of responsibilities. If you take the time to complete these exercises you will be pleasantly surprised at how easy it will be to prove you have the traits airlines deem desirable.

If you do not take the time to evaluate your skills and to become familiar with the flight attendant responsibilities, you could end up making a mistake that could cost you a job offer. To highlight the importance of doing these exercises let me share a story with you told to me by a Flight Attendant Interview Consultant.

Several years ago I received a phone call from a young woman who had interviewed with several airlines. However, she never received a job offer. As she put it, "When I send in my application I immediately get called for an interview, but can't seem to get them to offer me a job! What am I doing wrong?"

We made an appointment for a consultation. When she came to my office I knew it wasn't her grooming or poise that was the problem. She was tall, well-groomed, and attractive. In addition, she had applicable work experience including two years as a police dispatcher (no worries about her being able to handle an emergency!). I was puzzled.

I asked her to recall her interviews for me. I wanted to review what types of questions she had been asked, and how she had responded. As I listened I became more puzzled. Her responses sounded pretty good — until she mentioned that all the interviewers had made mention of the fact that she had never had a job where she had to wait on people (i.e., waitressing). Her response had been, "Well, I know that's not a big part of the job."

BINGO! This was why she had not been hired. #1: She went into an interview without a true understanding of the job and, #2: She gave the impression that she believed she would not have to spend a lot of time serving people.

When I explained this to her, she readily agreed. "Gosh, I grew up in a family of four kids. Being the oldest I had lots of time cooking and cleaning. I am not afraid of this type of work, but I can see where they might think I am!"

The next flight attendant interview she had, she was hired.

The following Self-Evaluation Exercises will give you an excellent understanding of a flight attendant's daily responsibilities, allow you to understand the reasoning behind the interviewer's questions, give you some examples of the Prepared vs Unprepared Applicant's Answers, and help you to uncover your own specific situations to discuss during the interview.

AS A FLIGHT ATTENDANT WHAT WILL MY DAILY ACTIVITIES BE?

(These are in order of FREQUENCY, NOT in order of IMPORTANCE. If these were listed in order of importance SAFETY would always be #1.)

- Meeting and greeting passengers (taking tickets and assisting with baggage, unaccompanied minors, parents with small children,and passengers needing special assistance).
- Assisting in maintaining an on-time performance (being on time for your check-in, making sure passengers are seated and baggage stored in an orderly, timely, and diplomatic fashion).
- Maintaining the safety of the aircraft cabin area (securing baggage, securing galley, checking passenger seating, etc.).
- Solving passenger problems and concerns (checking connections, assisting with medical emergencies, handling disruptive passengers, answering various questions concerning the flight).
- Checking catering/liquor.
- Conducting inflight meal and beverage services.

TRAITS AND SKILLS NEEDED

- Understanding the responsibilities of a flight attendant career.
- Dependability.
- Flexibility.
- Patience/Empathy.
- Communication Skills.
- Problem Solving Skills.
- Organizational Abilities.

BOTTOM LINE OF THE JOB

Your main goal as a flight attendant is to ensure a safe and stress-free flight for each passenger. You want to make sure that each passenger will choose to fly this airline again.

REVIEW YOUR SKILLS

Remember, it is your responsibility to PROVE to the interviewer that you have the traits that are required to be a professional flight attendant. Make sure you discuss specific jobs and/or situations that clearly show you possess these desired traits.

(CAUTION: In an interview you should only choose to give examples from your work life, not your personal life. For instance, you would not necessarily want to prove your empathy by discussing how you have stayed such good friends with your ex-spouse. These are personal issues that really have no place in an interview!)

KEEP IT TO TWO MINUTES

Your answers should not take longer than two minutes to tell. Stop for a moment and time two minutes. It's a long time!

SELF-EVALUATION WORKSHEET
Understanding the Flight Attendant Responsibilities

Interviewer's Reasoning: Does this person truly understand what it takes to be successful in this career? Will they be flexible enough to handle the uncertainty of the airline business? Are they independent and confident enough to move to another city where they might not know anyone?

Specific Questions

Tell us about yourself.
- Why do you want to be a flight attendant?
- Why do you want to work for this airline?
- What do you think would be the hardest part of a flight attendant's job?

In responding to these types of questions do not talk about what the airline can do for you ("I want to travel"). You must talk about the qualities you can bring to the airline. Discuss your customer service experience, your problem-solving abilities, and show yourself to be an independent person.

These types of questions will be asked time and again during the interviewing process. You may be asked to stand in front of a group and answer these questions. Or, you may be asked to answer more thoroughly in an individual interview. It is vital that you decide how you want to answer these questions prior to your interviews.

A prepared applicant would have researched the airline and would know what was expected of them as a flight attendant. A prepared applicant would understand the possibility of having to move, being away from home and family during holidays and weekends, and the need to be able to handle a lifestyle that requires tremendous flexibility.

For an example of a Prepared Applicant response review the previous example of the answer to the question: "Why do you want to be a flight attendant?"

Dependability

Interviewer's Reasoning: Does this person have a history of being on time and fulfilling job responsibilities? A flight attendant who is late for a flight or neglects to call in sick in time can dramatically impact a great number of flights, which costs the airline revenue and passenger goodwill.

Specific Background Question: How would your past employers rate your dependability?

Unprepared applicant: *"They would say I am very dependable."*

Prepared applicant: *"My employer would rate my dependability as very high. In fact,*

- *I received a bonus for never calling in sick at my current job.*
- *In the two years I have worked as a word processor for ABC Temporary Services I have never turned down an assignment, nor have I failed to complete a job."*

Situational Question: Can you describe a situation where someone was counting on you and you had to go out of your way to accommodate the person?

Unprepared applicant: *"I filled in for another waitress once."*

Prepared applicant: *"We have four full-time waitresses at the restaurant where I am currently working. Two of the waitresses called in sick at the last moment with the flu. My boss called me in on my day off and asked me to work. I had long-term plans for that day to take my niece to the zoo. However, my boss had always been very good to me so I really wanted to help him out. So, I promised my niece a trip to the zoo and a movie if we could postpone. I went in and worked a double shift."*

Ask Yourself - Dependability: Have I ever had to do extraordinary things in order to get to my job? (Were you the only one to show up at work during a snowstorm?)

Have I ever offered to chip in at work when things were busy? (Did you take a co-worker's shift when he called in sick unexpectedly?)

How many times have I called in sick at my current job?

Flexibility

Interviewer's Reasoning: Will this person be able to cope with the constant changes that occur at every airline? When you are dealing with a business that involves machinery, weather, and human beings you never really know what is going to happen. Trips get canceled or changed due to weather or mechanical problems. If a flight attendant becomes unhappy when these types of situations occur it causes more stress on everyone involved, passengers and co-workers included.

Specific Background Question: How do you feel about moving?
Unprepared applicant: *"I am ready to move."*
Prepared applicant: *"I understand fully that I will have to move. When I decided this was the career I wanted, I began to prepare myself financially for the training period and the move after training. I am excited about the prospect of moving to a new city."*

Situational Question: What would you do if you were on a two-day trip and were expecting to be home on Saturday night, but the trip had changed and now you wouldn't be home until Sunday night?
Unprepared applicant: *"I would do it."*
Prepared applicant: *"I understand that is part of the job. I have always made it a habit to have my address book with me at all times. I would simply contact anyone I needed to contact to tell them my work schedule had changed."*

Ask Yourself - Flexibility: Have I had to work overtime unexpectedly?
Have I ever had to fill in at a different office location that required me to change my regular routine?
Have I ever filled in for a co-worker?
Have I ever had to move to another city for a job?

Patience/Empathy

Interviewer's Reasoning: Does this person seem to care about people's problems? On a normal day a flight attendant can come in direct contact with hundreds of people. It is important that he is able to quickly read people's moods and sense when a problem could be developing. If you catch a problem early it is usually much easier to solve.

Specific Background Question: Tell me about a time when you thought a customer was being unreasonable.

Unprepared applicant: *"I can't think of a specific example, but I'm sure it has happened. I would just have to solve the problem."*

Prepared applicant: *"I worked as a receptionist in a doctor's office for two years. I remember one patient in particular who called us on a regular basis; she was a little bit of a hypochondriac. However, I also knew she lived alone and was probably lonely. I always took her complaints seriously. One day she wanted to be put right through to the doctor and wouldn't take "no" for an answer. I put her on hold and called the nurse on duty and explained I thought this patient just needed someone with a medical background to take two minutes to reassure her. The nurse took the call. This patient decided she didn't really need to speak directly to the doctor. It was obvious she just needed some reassurance, and I understood that."*

Situational Question: What would you do if you noticed an older gentleman passenger seemed to be upset and appeared to be crying?

Unprepared applicant: *"I would ask him if he needed anything."*

Prepared applicant: *"I would take him a glass of water and a tissue. I would very quietly kneel beside him and ask him if he needed anything else. If he wanted to talk I would listen. If he said "no," I would just leave him alone.*

Ask Yourself - Patience/Empathy: When have I had to work with people who I thought were being unreasonable? How did I handle the situation?

Have I ever offered to help out a co-worker who seemed to be having problems? How did I know this co-worker was having problems?

Have I ever had a co-worker or customer ask for my help with a problem? How did I handle the situation?

Communication Skills

Interviewer's Reasoning: A flight attendant regularly needs to communicate information to a variety of people in a very short period of time (explaining to a passenger why he must check his bag five minutes before departure). Also, flight attendants rarely work with the same people. For this reason it is important to have the ability to communicate concerns and approaches to problems clearly and quickly.

Specific Background Question: Tell me about a difficult customer you have had to deal with.

Unprepared applicant: *"In many of my jobs I have had to work with people who become upset. I know how to approach people and help them solve their problems."*

Prepared applicant: *"I was a resort hotel front desk receptionist for the last year. Early one morning a new guest who had just gotten off a long flight was extremely upset because his room was not ready. I listened to him for a few minutes and said something like, 'Oh dear, I am so sorry. Let me get right on it.' I then suggested that he go into our restaurant and have breakfast on us, and promised him I would let him know the room situation within 20 minutes. I also stored his luggage for him. He seemed satisfied with that. Although it took over an hour to get his room ready, it seemed to help that I kept him informed every 20 minutes or so."*

Situational Question: What would you do if you had a passenger who ordered a special meal and that meal had not been boarded?

Unprepared applicant: *"I would tell him that I was sorry. I would offer him a regular meal."*

Prepared applicant: *"Well, I would tell him that there really wasn't any excuse for the meal not to be on-board and that I realized he was upset. I would certainly make sure that he received a regular meal. If there were extra meals, perhaps I would be able to combine some meals to get him what he wanted. Also, I received a coupon for a free drink once because of a delay. Perhaps I could offer him that also."*

Ask Yourself - Communication: When have I been involved with a situation where the person was very angry and I diffused the situation?

Have I ever had to talk to someone about a difficult situation? (Did I have to counsel an employee who wasn't performing up to standard?)

Problem Solving

Interviewer's Reasoning: A flight attendant spends the whole day solving problems. It is imperative that she possess an ability to identify potential problems early and take steps to solve the problem before it turns into a huge problem.

Specific Background Question: Tell me about a difficult problem you had to solve quickly.

Unprepared applicant: *"Well, I really can't think of a specific problem. As a waitress when people don't like their food or their order is wrong, you have to make sure you get them their food back quickly."*

Prepared applicant: *"When I was a hotel concierge, my day was filled with problems that needed to be solved quickly. Guests lost their wallets, needed airline tickets, or a car unexpectedly, or perhaps had forgotten a birthday or anniversary and needed an appropriate gift immediately! One particular guest had a situation where his clothes had not come back from our dry cleaning service and he had a black-tie function to attend in less than two hours. I called a tuxedo rental shop down the street from our hotel and had them come over with several tuxedos he could choose from. The shop was very prompt and the hotel picked up the tab for the rental. Our guest went to his dinner and was no longer upset."*

Situational Question: What would you do if a passenger didn't want to check a bag that was too large to fit in the overhead bin or under his seat and it was 10 minutes before departure?

Unprepared applicant: *"I would tell him that it was the rule and there was nothing I could do about it."*

Prepared applicant: *"I would say something like, 'I understand perfectly that you are concerned about losing your bag, sir. I will walk it down to the baggage handler myself and make sure it gets on.' Then I would make sure that the bag did get on."*

Ask Yourself - Problem Solving: When have I solved a difficult problem at work?

Have I ever come up with a solution to a problem when no one else could?

Have I ever come up with a solution to a problem that was accepted by a group?

Organizational Abilities

Interviewer's Reasoning: Flight attendants are responsible for the entire cabin service. They are responsible for a wide variety of duties (boarding of passengers, checking of food and beverage supplies, the format of the inflight services, the safety of the cabin, and the deplaning of the passengers). If these responsibilities are not carried out in an organized manner it can result in a late flight and extremely unhappy passengers. In addition it can give the impression of an airline that does not properly train its staff, thus lowering passenger confidence.

Specific Background Question: Do you consider yourself an organized person? Please explain.

Unprepared applicant: *"Well, I make sure I have plenty of time to do my job. I prioritize pretty well."*

Prepared applicant: *"Sometimes you have to be creative! I worked for three years in retail sales for a small women's clothing store. Many times I would be the only person working in the store for hours at a time. Usually it wasn't a problem to be alone; however, sometimes it would be busy with customers in the store, new shipments coming in, and having the phones ringing. One of the big problems, especially when it was busy, was that the phone was in back of the store. I asked the owner of the store to put in a portable phone, then I kept it with me at all times. When the phone rang I could answer quickly and take a number to call the phone customer back. This way I didn't have to leave customers, plus the people calling felt taken care of because they knew I would be calling back soon."*

Situational Question: What would you do if the flight attendant you were working with kept forgetting to do things?

Unprepared applicant: *"I would remind her."*

Prepared applicant: *"Well, it would probably take me a couple of trips to notice she had this problem. I think I would probably just sit down with her before the flight and ask her what duties she wanted to perform and when. I would approach her as though I just needed to review these things. Perhaps that way, by thinking about these things in advance, she wouldn't forget so easily. I would also offer to help her with some of her duties."*

Ask Yourself - Organizational Abilities: How do I organize my life?

What specific steps do I take at my current job that help me stay ahead of schedule?

(NOTE: If you are a disorganized person, you need to start taking steps to improve in this area. Disorganization is the first step towards being late for a trip, or forgetting the required items you need to carry with you on your flights.)

It is easy to see the difference between the Unprepared Applicant and the Prepared Applicant. The most important difference is that the Prepared Applicant would be hired!

TYPES OF INTERVIEWS
The Group Interview

Airlines are on the lookout for prospective employees who will be assets for the company. Towards this goal, just about every major and regional airline utilize the group interview as part of their hiring process. Group interviews are used to select candidates who exhibit positive body language, have an excellent personal appearance, and show confidence in a group setting. This interviewing technique has proved to be a successful step in prioritizing the thousands of applicants pursuing a flight attendant career.

The group interview is normally the first interview you will encounter and can consist of up to 30 (or more!) applicants. There is usually more than one interviewer present. The applications are reviewed and any blanks or unclear answers are asked about at this time. These additions and clarifications will be noted on the application.

Each applicant will be given an opportunity to answer several questions. Additionally, each flight attendant hopeful may be asked to read aloud a short sample public address announcement. After the interviewers have completed their questioning, time is allowed for any questions the applicants may have.

When the group interview is over, normally those applicants who have been chosen to continue in the interviewing process are asked to stay behind while the other applicants are dismissed. However, each airline is different, so don't be surprised if the entire group is told that they will hear through the mail if selected to continue in the interviewing process.

Stand straight and tall when it is your turn to speak. Look around the room, SLOWLY, when you are speaking. Take your time and keep your voice strong. SMILE.

Also remember to pay attention when others are speaking. You are being watched through the whole interview session.

Group Exercises

There are very few moments in a flight attendant's day when she is NOT working as part of a team. So, it makes sense that the interviewers would want to see how applicants interact within a group setting.

One interview exercise is for applicants to be placed into small groups. They are then given a list of traits and responsibilities (e.g., dependable, safety-conscious, flexible) and asked to prioritize them in order of importance for a flight attendant position.

The interviewers are going to watch how each person interacts with others. Who is too aggressive? Who is too passive? Who is listening to others? Who is monopolizing the conversation?

In this type of situation you want to make sure that you show yourself to be a "quiet leader." Offer to take notes, suggest that everyone sit in a circle in order to include everyone, ask others for their input, listen carefully when others speak, get another chair if there are not enough to go around, say you agree with what someone has suggested, or gently disagree if someone has made a comment you oppose. If possible use people's names; this will show that you pay attention to others.

It is important to include yourself without talking over people or being pushy. If you find yourself in a group of loud, aggressive people, try raising your hand to signify your wish to speak instead of yelling over everyone.

Written Or Video Tests

Some airlines give short math tests (adding, subtracting, multiplying, dividing). These tests are to make sure an applicant has the ability to do basic math.

There may also be decision-making tests on video. Applicants watch a video that show several situations that a flight attendant could face on-board an aircraft. After the situation is presented, the video will pause and the applicant must choose the best answer to a series of questions. This test is to gauge an applicant's ability to think quickly and make mature, customer-service based decisions.

One-On-One Interviews

The one-on-one interview is normally the last interview you will
encounter. During this interview your appearance, poise, and ability to
communicate will be reviewed one more time.

The interview may last only 10 minutes or up to a half-hour.

Pay close attention to the interviewer's name and use his name at
least once during the interview. Don't be afraid to initiate shaking
hands. Don't sit down until invited. Listen carefully to the questions.
Maintain strong eye contact when you are listening or speaking. Keep
your body straight and quiet. SMILE!

STEP 3: PERSONAL PRESENTATION AND APPEARANCE

"You never get a second chance to make a first impression!" Your
appearance is a package. Your physical appearance, emotions, and
charm are all components of that package. Present the best you can be.
This doesn't mean your clothing must be expensive and ultra stylish. An
attractive, clean, neat, and flattering outfit is your goal. Male or female,
the same rules apply. Your appearance should call positive attention to you.

Airline hiring personnel are not looking for designer labels, theatrical
makeup, or "big hair." They are looking for a clean, neat, and
appropriate appearance. The most appearance-enhancing accessory you
can wear is your own natural personality and smile. Airlines devote a
tremendous amount of time and money to achieving their desired
appearance and presenting it to the flying public. Your appearance will
continue to be an issue throughout your career.

A small note on weight. Being overweight is no longer something to
be fired for, but don't believe for a moment that it isn't taken note of
during each and every interview. Interviewers are still on the lookout
for applicants with current or potential weight problems. Try to present
the best person you can be when applying for this still much-sought-
after career.

Clothing: Attractive, flattering, and simple. Sounds easy, right?
Figuring out what to wear can create more anxieties than figuring out
what to say! This is probably the number one question I hear: "What
should I wear?"

The applicant must wear something that she feels good in, has received genuine compliments on, and makes her feel comfortable. If all these elements exist, chances are your confidence will get a boost wearing it. Choose something with a little color to accent the main color choice. Navy blue has almost become the universal uniform color of the airlines. If you want to wear this color, that's great, but display some imagination with color accents. Remember, this is an interview, not a cocktail party or a football game. Dress appropriately. Once during a group interview of about 25 applicants, one male did indeed stand out. He arrived for his interview in a tuxedo! Not only did his choice of attire prove to be sadly wrong, his decision was considered so inappropriate that he was not passed on to a second interview. He looked great, but displayed poor judgment, something that the interviewers are on a constant lookout for.

Men: A clean shave and haircut is a must as is a suit and tie. Jewelry such as a watch is fine. Leave the earrings off. You want to be remembered for your answers, not your body piercing. Any visible tattoos are a definite NO! Give your shoes a once-over with the polish.

Women: You must wear an appropriate business dress or suit. Again, something that will flatter you. Do not wear pants. Although pants are acceptable in the workplace, a suit or dress is still the way a woman is expected to dress for a job interview. Add color to your selected outfit. If you are nervous, a little extra color around your face can help maintain your color and alleviate a "washed out" look. Pantyhose are a must. Shoes should be closed-toed and in good repair. Jewelry is a matter of taste but keep it simple and not extremely expensive. You should only wear one ring per hand and one pair of earrings. Do not wear dangle bracelets or multiple necklaces. Remember, each airline will have a strict uniform code that will limit you even more in your choices, so leave the extras at home.

Finally, make your clothes part of a consistent, non-verbal message about your identity, not your individuality. Once you are hired, the airline will outfit you with a uniform they have selected for the impression they want their customers to perceive. There is little room for creativity when in uniform and that's the way the company wants it! Always wear a smile — it goes with everything.

HOW NOT TO DRESS

Here are a few suggestions that may seem obvious, but are worth your attention.

Uncomfortably: Avoid clothing that is too small, too tight, too large, or could possibly come undone. For women, your heels should be no higher than 1 1/2 inches. Anything higher and you may wobble!

Suggestively: Women should not try to receive attention by wearing a plunging neckline or a skirt that is too short. Men should not wear a shirt unbuttoned to expose a hairy chest. You will come across as cheap and trying too hard. The reaction will be one of pity rather than admiration.

For Another Climate: Be aware of the weather conditions where the interview is being conducted and take the appropriate clothing. For example, in Dallas in the summer, air conditioning can make a room quite cool, even cold. You wouldn't want to wear a short-sleeved suit in those conditions.

Too Formally: Leave the cocktail and tuxedo attire at home.

Too Odorously: Don't forget the deodorant. Do NOT wear perfume or cologne. You never know who may be allergic.

As If You Don't Care: Airlines are looking to hire people who care. Show them by your appearance that you do care, and that you understand the importance of a professional appearance.

Your hair should be stylishly cut and clean. Make sure you keep your hair out of your eyes.

Fingernails should be clean and trimmed on the short side (no long fake nails please!). A clear polish or subdued, neutral nail color is acceptable.

Make sure your teeth are brushed and your breath is fresh. However, do not chew gum or eat hard candies or mints during the interview!

Make sure you do not have runs in your pantyhose or tears or spots on you clothing.

Airlines are continually working with their employees on their appearance and behavior. Some companies are publishing and distributing handbooks with titles such as *Impressions of Excellence* for their employees. Each airline strives for the highest standards and performance from their employees. If you don't come to an interview looking your best...what does that say about how you will dress for work?

ATTITUDE

Everyone has an attitude. Making sure you arrive for your interview with a positive one is your goal. Focusing on the positives that you have to offer an airline will prove to be a tremendous benefit. Being a flight attendant requires a unique blend of personal characteristics that can be displayed during your interviews. Attitude, when applied correctly and conservatively, can open or close the doors to your career.

Call attention to yourself by projecting yourself as a confident, reliable, and self-motivated person who has selected this airline to work for! During an interview is not the time for an air of superiority, however. By keeping your responses thoughtful and to the point, you will enable the interviewer to see the real you.

During an individual interview in Dallas, a young applicant was asked how she handled a difficult situation. She told of her arrival at Dallas-Fort Worth International Airport during a tremendous thunderstorm. The airport had been closed for some time thus causing her Dallas arrival time to be much later than she had anticipated. When she finally checked into her hotel room, she checked her garment bag and noticed it was unzipped. The skirt to her suit had fallen out and was gone. Quickly, she called a friend who lived in Dallas and they were able to get to a department store before closing time. She found something suitable to wear and returned to her hotel only to find the electricity off. Hoping the situation would be fixed by morning, she went to bed. When she awoke, still no electricity. She showered and washed her hair (in cold water), put on her makeup, and dressed — all in the dark of the early morning hours and without the benefit of a blow dryer! This young flight attendant hopeful was able to arrive at her interview on time with nerves intact and looking great! She could have given up at any point. Instead, as the numerous obstacles were thrown in her way, she persevered and thus demonstrated more than adequately that she was flight attendant material. This applicant did indeed proceed through the interview process successfully.

HANDSHAKE

A limp handshake accompanied by poor eye contact does not make a good first impression. It is better to have a handshake that is a bit too firm than too relaxed.

Here are some tips for a professional handshake. These tips are applicable whether you are meeting a man or a woman:

- Don't be afraid to extend your hand first.
- Make eye contact the whole time you are being introduced.
- Smile.
- Take the person's whole hand in yours. Make sure your thumb is aligned with the other person's wrist.
- Make sure you can feel the other person's whole hand. If you are touching all the pressure points, the handshake should feel firm without crushing bones.
- Hold the handshake for as long as it takes to say, "It's a pleasure to meet you." Then release.

Sweaty Hands: While you are waiting, keep your hands unclenched and let the air circulate around them.

Right before you meet someone, press your palm against your pants leg or skirt. The material will absorb a little bit of the excess moisture. Your hand may still be moist, but not dripping wet.

Smoking: Smoking could minimize your chances of being offered a flight attendant position. Whether you believe it or not, the smoke smell lingers on your skin and your clothes even when you think you are being careful. With today's airlines being smoke-free, no one is going to want to smell cigarette smoke on the flight attendant!

If you really want to pursue a flight attendant career, and protect your health, stop smoking now.

If you are unwilling to quit smoking, do not smoke, or be around smoke, in your interview clothing. Do not smoke the day of your interview.

STEP 4: CONDUCTING A MOCK INTERVIEW

Now, let's practice what you've learned. Conducting a mock interview will allow you to practice these techniques prior to the "real thing."

A videotaped mock interview is one of the most important and beneficial preparations you can make. Like any other important goal in your life if you are going to succeed you need to practice! A mock interview is a trial run of what you want to say during your interview, and an opportunity to view how others see you.

You will learn more from watching a half-hour video of yourself than you could ever learn in three weeks of constant critique from others. Watching yourself on videotape allows you to take a "third party" look at yourself. You will clearly see your mistakes as well as the things you do well!

You should do part of the mock interview standing up and part sitting down. This will simulate a group interview and a one-on-one interview.

Notice Your:

Eye Contact: When the interviewer is talking, you should be looking at him; when you are talking you should be looking at him. However, when you need to think, you may look away. Choose a "thinking spot" on the horizon (a wall switch, picture, etc.).

Body Language: Make sure you sit calmly in your chair. Keep your bottom up against the back of the chair with your feet flat on the ground. Do not cross your legs.

If you are standing don't shift your weight from foot-to-foot. Stand straight and keep your body calm.

Your goal is to not distract the interviewer with body twitches, fingering your hair, rubbing your face, etc.

Voice: You want your voice to be strong and even. Make sure you speak in complete sentences.

The Mock Interviewer: Pick someone whom you trust to give honest feedback. In order for him to fully understand the learning process you are going through, have him read, or at least skim, this book.

Dress: Set the stage to mirror the interview atmosphere. Wearing your interview suit will allow you to really feel as if you are in an interview. If you don't want to wear your interview suit, at least wear business attire: a coat and tie (for men) and a skirt and blouse (for women).

Stage: Once again, set the stage correctly. You should sit in a straight-backed chair. Have the interviewer sit next to the camera. You should be the only person seen on camera.

Camera View: Be careful of the lighting in the room. Make sure you have the light straight ahead of you. Do not have a lamp in back of you or to the side as this will place your face in shadow. Have your interviewer sit to the side of the camera. You should always be looking at the interviewer, not the camera.

When you are standing up make sure your entire body can be seen. When you are sitting down the camera should give a clear view of you from the knees up. You want to be able to view your entire body stance. A good way to critique body language is to ask the interviewer if he was distracted by something you were doing (fidgeting in your chair, arranging your hair, etc.).

Questions: The interviewer should select the questions at random. (Use the questions listed in the Self-Evaluation Worksheet.) Also, provide your interviewer with a copy of your resume to help stimulate more specific questions concerning your particular background. The mock interview should be at least one-half hour long and include questions from all the categories listed in the Self-Evaluation Worksheet.

Review: After the mock interview, ask your interviewer for his initial reactions. Discuss how you felt and where you sensed you did well or not so well. Do your critiques match? If not, pay special attention to the areas of disagreement and perhaps get a third opinion. It is important to remember that you must be open to constructive criticism. Do not get angry with your mock interviewer for giving his opinion, especially since you asked for it! If you feel it is an exceptionally harsh critique, ask someone else to do another mock interview to get a second opinion.

After your initial discussion, review the tape together. Stop the tape whenever you see a problem and discuss ways to improve.

Make sure you take notes while watching the interview tape.

Additional Mock Interviews: Although this is a necessary and helpful exercise, it is important not to overdo it. Conducting numerous mock interviews will only cause you to become unrealistic in your critique. You will begin to look for perfection, which is impossible for any of us. Do no more than two mock interviews prior to a specific interview.

One mock interview should be done at the beginning of your preparation — perhaps after working through this book once. The second interview should be done two or three days after you have had time to scrutinize your initial responses and work through the rough areas.

Chapter 7

Common Applicant Concerns

If you can eliminate these common mistakes your chances for success will soar!

COMMON MISTAKES:

Being Late: Airlines are very inflexible when it comes to time. They have to be! One of the top products they sell is on-time departures and arrivals. A probationary flight attendant will not be given a second chance if she is late. Don't expect any grace period from the interviewing team either. Don't rely on hoping you know the location of the interview. Drive there before your interview date. Locate parking and have the correct change to pay any parking fees. Remember, depending on the city and time of day, traffic density could be a cause for delay. Give yourself more time than you think you need. Arrive early. Take the extra time for last minute touch-ups on your personal appearance or to look over your paperwork.

Speaking Poorly of Others: Don't! Especially of past or current employers. It is social and professional bad manners. The interviewers do not want to hear of problems you've dealt with in your past jobs except in response to a specific question. Flight attendants are often heard above the sounds of the airplane in flight. Believe it or not, all the way from the back galley to row five, your private conversation can often be heard! If you speak poorly of others during an interview, will you also speak poorly of the airline in front of the passengers? Treat everyone you meet with respect and courtesy.

Once we were shorthanded while interviewing at a remote location. I not only checked in the applicants, I followed them into the interview room and conducted the group interview! If someone had treated me poorly during the check-in process, how could I possibly consider that person for a customer-service-oriented professional career? Never forget your manners!

Poor Verbal Presentation: Being comfortable speaking in front of people is a necessity for a flight attendant. Having the ability to relay safety information, give directions in an emergency, or simply inform a plane full of passengers of what is on the menu is a big part of the job. You must speak in a clear, confident voice. Keeping a train of thought without fillers such as "umm" and "ah" is important in conveying the desired professional and authoritative image. Anyone listening to a public address (and on an airplane they do listen) knows how infuriating it can be to hear someone trip and stammer through a message. During the course of the interviews, you may be asked to read a prepared announcement. Most airlines now require flight attendants to read (rather than memorize) the appropriate announcements while at work; however, practicing your delivery will always be beneficial. When practicing, maintain good posture without leaning, foot shuffling, or swaying side to side. Take your time, speak clearly, and maintain good eye contact.

Unnecessary Distractions: Do not carry into the interview any unnecessary extras such as a water bottle; leave it in the car. A cellular phone must be turned off and out of sight at all times. If you need to make a call, wait until a break to do so. A ringing phone is not welcomed at any time. A pager should be kept out of sight and turned off as well.

Not Having the Correct or Complete Paperwork: Flight attendants are responsible for a large amount of paperwork. Sometimes even their pay sheets must be completed by hand and personally submitted in order to receive pay. The company puts great emphasis on filling out the flight manifest, liquor counts, and incident reports correctly! If you cannot appear at your interview with your paperwork prepared, you will leave the impression that you will not be able to handle the paperwork responsibilities required of a flight attendant.

Messy Paperwork: Are you presenting the complete "you" on paper? Before you have even walked into the room and smiled your brightest smile, your presentation on paper has been critiqued. Check and double-check your work for: spelling, neatness, correct grammar, and above all, following the directions. Clear, straightforward answers are essential. Once you feel you have done your best, have a trusted friend review your entire interview paperwork before it is sent to the airline. Your application and paperwork will be the first impression you make upon the airline — present your best.

Not Listening: Don't be so prepared with answers that you fail to hear the questions. No matter how much help you may have received from a current or past employee concerning what to expect in the interviews, questions will change! Let the interviewer complete each question before you answer. When asked, "Tell me of a difficult situation you recently encountered at work..." an applicant I know jumped right in with a blow-by-blow account of a problem he had experienced with a customer that resulted in an unpleasant ending. If the applicant had allowed the interviewer to finish "...and how you were able to make the customer happy," he probably would not have used that example. He had already shown his hand and changed the complexion of the question. Don't let this happen! Do not plan your response before the question is completed. By preparing your answer during the question, you could possibly miss the entire point of the question. Don't read anything into a question, facial expression, or gesture made by the interviewer. This could destroy your train of thought and necessitate a "Would you repeat the question?" query. If you constantly ask for questions to be repeated, this is a sign of not listening. Also, don't use this as a delay tactic. Take your time and say what you mean. By listening, considering the question, and responding appropriately you will give the impression of being well-organized.

Giggling or Joking: Some people react to nervousness by giggling. Don't! This type of response will be judged as juvenile and inappropriate. If your idea of putting someone at ease is to tell a joke, resist the urge. It is not the applicant's responsibility to set the mood or direction of the interview. You and the interviewer may have opposite ideas of what's funny. This doesn't mean a sense of humor isn't appropriate. If something funny is said or happens, by all means, smile, or laugh appropriately. A smile is always acceptable and appreciated.

Poor Physical Presentation: Physical presentation is more than the clothing and shoes you wear. Your good health, body language, and grooming are all components of the entire package you want to present. Don't forget eye contact! Do not look at the ground or your hands while speaking or listening. A confident person will look you in the eye and smile. These items are all very important parts of the impression you want to convey.

Give your clothing one last check. Wrinkled, soiled, falling hem, slip showing, or button missing? Correct the problems or change the outfit. This is not the time to let a small inconvenience create the wrong impression.

If you don't normally wear makeup, now is not a good time to experiment. Ask for professional help. Department stores offer wonderful opportunities for a make-over at no cost to you. Set up an appointment and go! If you don't like the way the free make-over looks, you may want to invest in a professional makeup lesson. You may end up preferring your way of applying makeup, but you need to have something to compare your style to. On an airplane, the lighting is harsh and the need for more color is necessary. A trained makeup professional will be a big help in addressing application concerns and color coordination.

Also, do not chew gum or candy during an interview!

Not Sharing Your Attention: Chances are that there will be more than one person involved in your interviews. Be certain to rotate your attention to include each person. If one interviewer asks the question, make eye contact with both. Thank both persons (by name) when you leave. A handshake is fine if you are the only applicant in the room. The group interview doesn't lend itself to that opportunity, so don't plan on one.

To sum it up: Be on time, be yourself, be courteous, and be prepared!

COMMON QUESTIONS:

1) What should I wear?

Refer to Chapter Five. Remember that what you wear will make a statement about you that will leave a lasting impression. Neat, clean, and well-groomed is the goal.

Take a small/medium size purse/briefcase. Make sure it has a shoulder strap so your hands will be free to accept paperwork or to shake hands. Also, always take a pen and pencil and a small pad of paper with you. You want to appear prepared.

2) What if I'm late for my interview?

NEVER be late for an airline interview. If you are, chances are you won't be admitted to the interview. All that work you went through to portray the proper image and high level of responsibility required to be a flight attendant has flown out the window. You will have to reapply. Airplanes wait for no one, nor does the interview process.

3) When will I hear about the results of my interview?

Every airline is different. You may hear before you leave, you may receive a call that evening at home, or you may be notified by mail. If you make it through the entire interviewing process, you will most likely be notified by mail. Make certain they have your current phone number and address on file.

4) Can I find out the results?

No. You will not be able to reach an interviewer. You will have to wait to be contacted by the airline.

5) If I'm not successful, can I find out what I did wrong?

Chances are-no. If you can sit down and honestly critique what you said during the interview, and HOW you said it, you will have a good idea on where you need improvement. Don't give up! Many, many flight attendants had to interview two, or even three times before being successful. If you are unable to figure out what went wrong on your own, it might be time to invest in some interview consulting. (Please see information on Cage Consulting at the back of this book.)

6) During a group interview how can I attract the interviewer's attention towards me without being obnoxious?

Smile!

Take Your Time! When it is your turn to tell the group about yourself, or to answer a question, take your time. Speak clearly and slowly.

Listen! Not only to the interviewer but to what the other applicants are saying.

Look Professional! Your interview attire and your hair and makeup say a lot about you. Make sure you look terrific.

Speak Up! If in a group situation, add to the conversation. BUT BEWARE—do not speak over others, or dominate the conversation. Listen to what others have to say.

Ask Questions! If you are asked if you have any questions, make sure you ask one! Good subjects could be about training, or new aircraft orders, or how many flight attendants will be hired during the year.

7) Can I continue to work during initial training?

As a general rule, no. Once you are offered employment and your training begins, you will be heavily engulfed in eight-hour days for six to nine weeks. Your attendance may be required for six days a week, with daily hours perhaps exceeding eight. This is similar to any educational endeavor and your out-of-class time will be spent studying. So, don't plan on working another job during training.

8) What if I cannot attend the initial interview?

Call to reschedule as soon as possible. Be prepared to wait for a future interview date. But, never forget, seniority begins when you start class. Any delay in your hiring date can mean the difference in domicile location and your seniority in applying for trips, vacation, etc. Timing is very important!

9) Am I required to join a union?

Joining a union is generally not a requirement of employment. Each airline is different. You will be informed during your training if you have union representation available and specifically what membership entails.

However, when there is a union representation, the majority of flight attendants do join.

10) What can I do if am unsuccessful?

It is important not to try to "learn as you go." When you are not selected for employment you normally have to wait at least six months before you can reapply. It is important to do some interview preparation prior to any of your interviews. If you have already attended some flight attendant interviews and were unsuccessful, you need to do some serious review of each of the unsuccessful interviews. If you cannot figure out what you did wrong on your own, then it is time to contact a Flight Attendant Interview Consultant who can help you discover what is going wrong. Or, a flight attendant who has some experience in flight attendant interviewing may be able to provide you with some insight (if you are lucky enough to know someone!).

11) I just get so nervous before an interview. What can I do to become more relaxed?

First of all remember that you are human. Flight Attendant Interviewers are not expecting perfection, just an outgoing, well-groomed, poised individual.

Following the advice in this book will be of tremendous help. Doing a mock interview will allow you to work through the rough areas and organize your thoughts prior to the actual interview.

Remember to get enough sleep in the days before your interview. Avoid alcoholic beverages several days prior to the interview. Make sure you have plenty of time to travel to the interview site. Eat a light meal prior to the appointment, forego the coffee or colas (anything with caffeine).

Being nervous is a part of being human. Just remember that everyone else is a little anxious too!

Notes

In Conclusion

This book was not written with the intention of furthering the glamorous job myth. Being a flight attendant is a very demanding occupation.

Airlines are very specific and selective when it comes to who will wear their flight wings. Currently only 3% of the applicants successfully complete the intensive interview process. How well you interview is the key!

Using the suggestions in this book should help many of you gain employment with your chosen airline after only one round of interviews. However, others may need to sharpen their technique and return for a second, third, or possibly a fourth attempt before the reality of a flight attendant career is realized.

Don't be discouraged if you have to return and try again! Many current flight attendants have had to take that route. I had always been told by friends and family that I was too short to be a flight attendant. I persevered and found a wonderful airline where I met all of their requirements. Retaining a positive attitude, and refusing to give up, often renders a positive result.

I am always interested in hearing from you. Please drop a note (care of Cage Consulting) and let me know if you found this book helpful, or if you have suggestions for improvement. Good luck and happy flying!

Becky S. Bock

GLOSSARY

"A" FLIGHT ATTENDANT: Most senior flight attendant in the crew and usually in charge of the organization of the flight service and flight attendants. Also called Lead flight attendant or Senior flight attendant.

ABORT: To halt the process of takeoff or landing.

AFT: Rear section of aircraft.

A/C: Aircraft.

ARM THE DOORS: Securing the evacuation slide to the exit door. This is done after the airplane has pushed back from the gate. In case of emergency, the door could be opened and an evacuation slide would inflate allowing passengers and crew to slide safely to the ground.

ATA: Actual Time of Arrival.

ATC: Air Traffic Control. Air Traffic Controllers work in the airport towers and control centers and oversee most airplane traffic.

BASE: City in which a crew member originates and ends all trips.

BID: A request of choice to fly specific monthly schedules or individual trips. Awarded according to seniority.

BOARD: To accomplish the process of loading passengers aboard the aircraft.

BRIEFING: Pre-trip communication between working crew members conducted by the captain and lead flight attendant.

BULKHEAD: The wall dividing sections of the aircraft such as between first class and coach class.

CABIN: Inside of aircraft - passenger section and working area for flight attendants.

CHECK-IN: The time a flight crewmember must notify the scheduling department that they are at the airport and ready for their assigned trip. Normally this is one hour prior to departure of the trip.

COCKPIT: The pilots working area (Flight Deck).

COCKPIT CREW: The pilots.

COMMUTE: The process of getting to a domicile in order to begin a trip.

CREW: The total complement of pilots and flight attendants required to work a flight.

CREW LIST: A listing of the names of the flight attendants and pilots.

CREW LEGALITIES: see legalities.

DEADHEAD: To move from one city to another by air or ground, in uniform, and at company expense.

DECOMPRESSION: Loss of pressurization.

DELAY: Unplanned interruption of flight schedule.

DEPLANE: To leave the aircraft.

DEREGULATION: When the government no longer regulated where airlines could fly, or how much they could charge. All cities are now open for any airline to offer service.

DIVERT: To land at a different airport than the original destination. An airplane may have to divert when the weather is bad at the original destination.

DOMESTIC: Within the continental United States.

DOMICILE: City in which a crew member begins and ends all trips.

ETA: Estimated Time of Arrival.

ETD: Estimated Time of Departure.

FAA: Federal Aviation Administration.

F/A: Flight Attendant.

FAR: Federal Aviation Regulation.

FLT: Flight.

FLIGHT TIME / FLIGHT HOURS: Actual or scheduled time in-the-air for pay purposes.

FURLOUGH: A reduction of personnel. Layoff.

GALLEY: The kitchen area of an aircraft.

GROUND PERSONNEL: Company employees other than flight crew members (i.e. ticket agents, gate agents, ramp agents).

HOLDING PATTERN: When an airplane is unable to land at their destination airport due to weather or traffic delays then the airplane must be put in a "holding pattern." Air Traffic Controllers instruct the pilots to maintain a certain altitude above the airport. The airplane circles the airport at this altitude until landing becomes possible. A normal and common procedure.

ILLEGAL: It is sometimes stated that the crew is "illegal." For example, this could mean that due to a delay they were not able to get the minimum rest period required by law, or perhaps because of a weather problem the crew has been on duty for too long.

INBOUND: Arriving crew and aircraft.

INTERPHONE: Phones located at the forward, aft, and cockpit sections of an airplane. Used for crew communications.

INITIAL TRAINING: The first training class for new-hires. Must be successfully completed before performing duties on a revenue flight.

INTERNATIONAL: Outside the connected United States.

JETWAY: The covered walkway that extends from the terminal to the aircraft providing access for boarding and deplaning.

JUMPSEAT: A designated seat for a flight attendant in uniform utilized for takeoff and landing.

LAYOVER: Time between flights or rest hours at hotels. (also written as L/O)

LEAD: See "A" Flight Attendant.

LEG: A flight segment from one city to another.

LEGALITIES: The FAA, airline, and union rules which state such items as mandatory rest periods between flights, maximum numbers of hours to be flown per month, etc.

LINE OF FLYING: The sequence of trips (or days on in the case of reserves) you are awarded each month.

LINE HOLDER: Someone who has a specific assignment of trips for the month. Someone NOT on reserve.

MANIFEST: The list of passengers' names and seat assignments, non-revenue passengers, special meal requests, unaccompanied minor children, and final head count.

MANUAL: The flight attendant manual that must be carried by each flight attendant when on duty. The information in the manual encompasses FAA regulations and airline flight attendant specific regulations and responsibilities.

MISSED FLIGHT: Failure to report in a timely manner for any portion of the flight assignment.

NON-REVENUE: (Also called non-rev, stand-by, or space available.) An airline employee, travel agent, or eligible family member who flies on a standby basis for a nominal fee.

OVERHEAD: Compartments for luggage storage.

OVERNIGHT: Company paid on-duty hotel time away from home. See "Layover."

ON-CALL: When a flight attendant must be available to be called by scheduling for a trip. This term is used primarily when you are a reserve flight attendant.

PA: Passenger announcements made to passengers by airline personnel.

PAX: Passengers.

PRE-BOARDS: Physically impaired, elderly, unaccompanied minors, government escorts, families with small children, or anyone needing extra time to board. Allowed to board aircraft prior to general boarding.

QUICK CALL: When a flight attendant is called "at the last minute" to be scheduled for a flight. This usually occurs when another flight attendant calls in sick at the last minute, or misses a check-in.

RAMP: Area around terminal where aircraft are parked, serviced, and loaded prior to flight.

RECURRENT TRAINING: Once a year, one or two-day training to maintain currency in emergency, first aid, CPR, etc. FAA mandated.

RESERVE: A flight attendant without a definite schedule of flights for the month who may be called out to work a flight or series of flights on short notice.

RON: Remain Over Night. See "Layover."

RUNWAY: Designated area for takeoffs and landings.

SATELLITE BASES: Bases that are staffed with dramatically less employees than larger bases.

SENIORITY / SENIOR: Years of service with the company based upon date of hire.

SCHEDULING / CREW SCHEDULING: The department in charge of coordinating specific flight assignments for flight attendants and pilots. They handle reserve assignments, sick calls from flight attendants and pilots. Normally there is a separate department for flight attendants and pilots.

SIGNALS: Chimes are used as signals from the cockpit to the flight attendants. Chimes are also used to signify passenger needs. The chimes can be heard in the passenger cabin. For example the cockpit may sound two chimes which means that landing is imminent. One chime usually sounds when a passenger presses a flight attendant call button.

TAXI: Aircraft movement from the ramp to the active runway for takeoff or from the runway to the ramp area after landing.

THE CALL: see "on call"

TRIP PAIRING: (The language may vary from airline to airline.) A series of flights and appropriate layovers scheduled to be accomplished from check-in to check-out at a flight attendant's domicile.

TURBULENCE: Bumpy air in flight caused by weather, mountains, or wind currents.

UNACCOMPANIED MINOR: A child under age 12 traveling alone.

WINGS: A pin with the company insignia/name. Must be worn with the uniform.

Books & Services Offered By Cage Consulting, Inc.

CAREER SERVICES

Flight Attendant Interview Preparation - Individual or Seminar
Professional Pilot Job Search Services
Career Search Services for Business Professionals

BOOKS BY CAGE CONSULTING

(Please add $3.00 for shipping and handling)

Can You Start Monday? A 9-Step Job Search Guide - Resume to Interview
by Cheryl A. Cage $14.95
A different type of job search guide. In addition to a step-by-step program which guides you through writing a resume and cover letters, networking, interviewing, etc., this book is filled with real-life examples and a heavy dose of optimism and motivation. A silent mentor for any job applicant.

Checklist for Success: A Pilot's Guide to the Successful Airline Interview (revised for 1998)
by Cheryl A Cage $31.00
Over 12,000 copies sold!
"All the advice I could provide is contained in this book. Your careful reading and study of this material, although it cannot guarantee success, will certainly enhance your chances." W.H. Traub, Vice-President, United Airlines Flight Standards and Training (Ret. 1997).

Flight Plan to the Flight Deck: Strategies for a Pilot Career
by Judy A. Tarver $16.95
A must read for anyone pursuing a professional pilot career. Written by a former manager of pilot hiring for a major U.S. Airline, this book is filled with advice that will allow a pilot to take years off the time it takes to achieve their dream.

Welcome Aboard: Your Career as a Flight Attendant
by Becky S. Bock $14.95
This information-packed book will answer all your questions about the flight attendant interview process and the career itself. By using the advice contained in this book, your chances of gaining employment as a flight attendant will soar!

CONTACT US!

Nationwide toll free: 1-888-899-CAGE

Locally in Denver, CO Metro Area: 1-303-799-1991

Fax: 1-303-799-1998

Website address: http://www.cageconsulting.com

Send correspondence to Cage Consulting, Inc.,

PO Box 460327, Aurora, Colorado 80046-0327